Behind the
Sixteen
Doors

Patti Neri

Copyright © 2024 Patti Neri
All rights reserved
First Edition

Fulton Books
Meadville, PA

Published by Fulton Books 2024

ISBN 979-8-89427-435-5 (paperback)
ISBN 979-8-89427-436-2 (digital)

Printed in the United States of America

To those whose lives have been utterly derailed
but find the courage to get back on track.

Chapter 1

During her usual Sunday morning run through the nearby community park, Dr. Claire Thompson can feel her sixty-four-year-old leg muscles cramping, and her pulse rate is markedly increasing too rapidly. Along the leaf-littered pathway just ahead, she stops under the mature sugar maple tree nearly devoid of its colorful pointed leaves to give herself a necessary break.

As she sips on her fortified water in between stretches, she curiously observes there are only sixteen leaves left hanging from the alternating branches above—*sixteen*, the same number of her first-period high school students.

Claire studies the remaining autumn leaves while she hydrates and rests her body. She sees how unique they are in their colorful appearance but knows how similar the leaves must have looked when they first budded in the spring. She wonders what caused each of the leaves to turn into their own particular shade of orange, green, brown, or yellow. Within her own thoughts, she tries to account for the unique changes. *Was it the environment or the elements or just a predetermined act of nature?*

After a quick respite, Claire continues her run but atypically stops at the top of the hill and looks back at the lone sugar maple tree before it's completely gone from her sight. She notices that several of the sixteen lingering leaves are now swirling toward the ground where they will join the countless other maple leaves layered on top of each other.

Once they land, they will become indistinguishable from the previously fallen leaves as if they are losing their own individual identity. The same thing will happen to my sixteen troubled teenagers, unless I can figure out how to get through to them. Claire tries to rationalize her anxious thoughts. *Somehow, I need to get them to open up. I need their voices to be heard; otherwise, I'm never going to be able to help them, and they'll become lost in the system like so many high school teenagers before them.*

Claire was vacillating with uncertainty when she was first approached about developing this experimental high school class. Before she retired from her previous employment, Dr. Claire Thompson had been a suicide and acute trauma therapist for adult individuals who couldn't cope with their own troubled and stressful lives. Her patients had closed themselves off from their coworkers, family, and friends for one reason or another. She would lead group sessions so her disconcerted patients would be able to work as a team to open up and share their innermost feelings, and Dr. Claire became very successful and renowned for her specialized and unconventional methods of working with her patients through group therapy sessions.

Since her retirement a few years prior, Claire had been working part time as a substitute teacher for the local area high school. Because of her background, she was approached by the local district school board to pilot an unorthodox program for above-average intellectual students who had suddenly shut down—similar in actions to persons dealing with traumas. Their district's educational facilities were already prepared to deal with schoolwide traumas because of the ever-increasing number of school shootings and bomb threats nationwide, but these select sixteen students were individuals dealing with suspected personal traumas—whether acute, chronic, or complex was unknown.

Claire reluctantly agreed to spearhead this innovative class, but only if she was allowed to retain doctor/patient confidentiality and did not have to report her findings to the district, the school, the parents, or the authorities if she believed it would be detrimental to her students. She also requested that each of the troubled teenagers must agree, of their own volition, to take part in the experimental group therapy classroom.

Behind the *Sixteen* Doors

On her remaining mile run home, Claire tries to figure out a way for her students to express themselves using a common focus such as that sugar maple tree in the park, yet unique like its multi-hued leaves. She goes over and over former project ideas and group sessions in her head, but none of them were viable exercises for her special group of sixteen students. Claire knows she will only be able to help them if they open up to her but also knows she needs to proceed with caution and patience because she still has no idea what triggered their downfall.

Claire's rambling thoughts continue to center on her stressed teenagers as she nears the end of her run. *These sixteen high school students are all gifted, intelligent, and creative individuals but have shut themselves off from everyone they cared about, their school, and themselves. They are as unique as the colorful fall leaves on the sugar maple tree or the pastel-painted doors on the townhouses across the street.*

While retrieving her apartment key from her back pocket, Claire experiences a eureka moment and quickly looks back toward all the distinctively colored doors. She enthusiastically smiles when she believes she has finally come up with an ingenious and creative idea to get her students to open themselves up.

Claire doesn't even shower before pulling out several overly stuffed photo albums from her tall antique cabinet in her guest bedroom. She sits on the bed and chuckles out loud as she flips through the first book and sees some of the school-aged pictures of her two sons, Paul and Chase, who are now in their late thirties, but melancholy smiles when she turns to several photos taken of her with her late husband, Peter. After taking a few moments to be nostalgic, Claire recalls the task at hand and quickly flips through more album pages. After looking through almost her entire collection, Claire starts to become frustrated because she still hasn't found what she is looking for.

She grabs the remaining few photo albums to look through and finally feels a sense of relief when the last book she opens looks promising. This sorted collection of pictures shows Paul and Chase as young adults standing with her future daughter-in-law, Anna, on the deck of a *Windstar* cruise ship. Claire is ecstatic when she spots what she has been searching for—a couple photographs of distinctive doors taken by the three of them while on a family trip to Italy, Monaco, and France.

Claire thumbs through more pages and removes several additional pictures of uniquely styled doors. By the time she has finished going through the album, Claire has only amassed thirteen photographs of extraordinary doors taken on one of their Mediterranean trips. She carefully looks behind other pictures to make sure she has accumulated all of them and confirms those are all the captured door photographs she's going to find from this family trip to Europe. She stores the perused albums back in the cabinet and gathers up the pictures off the guest bed to take with her.

While finally showering after her run and her album search, she tries to figure out where she will find the most unusual or distinguishable doors in the surrounding area so she can take at least three more door photos today. After she finishes getting cleaned up and dressed, Claire decides to take a quick drive through town to look at some of the century-old architecture currently housing the local businesses and to possibly consider checking out one or two of the local churches as well.

Along one of the side streets heading into town, Claire sees a boarded-up house with an exposed, peeling front door. She gets out of her car with her digital camera and moves in as close as possible without trespassing in order to photograph the neglected wood and broken-glass entry. She races back to her car pleased with her discovery, now eager to find a couple more. Claire parks her car downtown and walks the four-block business district where she locates and photographs numerous unique doors she had regrettably never noticed until now. *These old buildings are like works of art,* she thinks to herself as she marvels at their architecture and ornamentation featured throughout the historic downtown.

Claire returns to her car and drives to the oldest church in town—her former place of worship. She cautiously approaches the front of the church on foot and takes a photo of the arched, carved double doors right before the second Sunday service is about to end.

Behind the *Sixteen* Doors

She hurries to get back into her car to avoid the parishioners and clergy already beginning to trickle out of the church.

Next, Claire travels down several side streets but doubles back so she can take a photo of the large bay doors at the local fire station before deciding she has photographed enough additional doors for her students' selection tomorrow. She eagerly returns home to print off the newly collected images.

Across her bedspread, Claire lines up her old and new printouts in several rows. There are now twenty-three door photographs so her students will have extras to choose from as well. Looking at all the four by six–inch photographs, she decides they are way too small in size for the big impact she wants to make with her sixteen students, so she'll have to enlarge them before her first class tomorrow. She knows from past experience that using the busy faculty copier before school is not a guarantee she'll get them all finished before the first period begins, so Claire quickly gathers up all the photographs, her camera, and her purse and heads back out to her car. She pulls up to the nearby high school main parking lot and then sends a text message to Brad, one of the weekend maintenance staff and a former high school classmate, to let her into the school.

"Be right there." He texts his response.

Claire eagerly waits at the main door for Brad to let her in. While standing there, she decides to take a picture of the oversized school door since she doesn't have any doors made entirely of clear glass as one of the choices. She's looking at the digital photo when Brad knocks on the floor-to-ceiling glass panel next to the front door. Claire chuckles when she sees him posing for a picture so she obliges by taking his snapshot through the glass panel.

"What brings you here on a fine Sunday morning?" Brad inquires while holding open the door for her. "Did you just stop by to see your old friend?"

Claire gives Brad a friendly hug and smiles. "Wish that was the only reason because it's always nice seeing you, Brad, but I also need to enlarge some pictures for my first-period class tomorrow," Claire replies. "I thought it would be easier doing it now rather than fighting with the other faculty over the use of the copier in the morning before class. I'll text you when I'm ready to leave if that's okay with you."

"Fine with me. I plan on being here all day anyway, so take your time." Brad waves her on and heads back down the main hall in the opposite direction to return to his interrupted routine maintenance schedule.

Claire proceeds to the faculty supply and equipment room to begin with and finds some heavier semigloss stock paper. She mulls it over and decides to print the pictures on the stock paper rather than use the more expensive and thicker photo paper. After running her enlarged copies, Claire is quite pleased with the way the letter-sized color prints are turning out and starts to line them up again to view them and to make sure the ink is completely dry before moving them to her classroom. Next, she finds a compatible printer cable cord in the supply cabinet and loads the glass door photograph directly into the copier from her camera. It will be the final door she adds to the "Behind the Door" project collection.

To ensure the printer ink won't smudge, Claire decides to be overly cautious and waits about ten minutes longer than usual for the enlargements to dry completely before she stacks one printout on top of another in order to carry them to her classroom. While she's killing some time waiting, she elects to play a little game with herself and grabs a sheet of paper and a pen. She writes down the first names of her sixteen students and tries to guess who will choose which door to reflect themselves and their issues, even though she still doesn't have the slightest clue what is affecting any one of them. Claire folds up her list, based purely on her past observations of her students, and puts it into her purse for safekeeping until her students make their own individual selections.

Once she double-checks the dryness of the copies, she carefully stacks them and carries them into her classroom. She begins randomly hanging them up along the wall using the existing clips and permanently installed horizontal wire wrapping around most of the classroom for temporary display purposes. Claire takes a step back and smiles with approval while observing all the enlarged door pictures she has exhibited along three of the walls. Before

Chapter 2

As she's unnecessarily readjusting some of the colored door prints while anxiously waiting for the first bell to sound, the high school principal knocks on her door and then steps inside her classroom.

"What's all this?" he curiously asks while pointing to the door photographs on display.

Claire optimistically responds, "Just a little project for these students that will hopefully shed light on their individual issues."

"I hope you're right. Some of the other faculty members are losing patience with these students in their own classes because of their lack of ambition and apathetic attitudes. They find their negative traits quite disruptive to their other more attentive students. With your specialized background, we're hoping you might be able to change things around for them. Actually, we're counting on it."

He walks around the room while continuing, "By the way, Claire, any chance you can cover in the counselor's office today? I know you usually just sub for teachers after this class, but I could really use you today and tomorrow in that position. It will only be through the lunch period for both days."

"Sure. That shouldn't be a problem. I'll head over there right after my first period class." Claire then adds, "But please make sure the door is unlocked this time or give me a key to get into the counselor's office."

He pulls a key from his pocket and grimaces while handing it to her. "Glad you reminded me. I would have forgotten to give it to you again." The principal smiles and inquisitively takes another curious look at the unusual door photographs hanging around the room she leaves her classroom, she closes her eyes and prays her newest "Behind the Door" project will finally help her *sixteen* break out of their shells.

Behind the *Sixteen* Doors

before leaving. He knows better than to question her further about her projects and teaching methods.

The first bell sounds, and her students slowly start filing in the classroom. All sixteen are thankfully present by the time the second bell rings.

With a renewed excitement in her voice, Dr. Claire greets her first class that Monday morning and points out all the pictures of doors hanging around the room once they are seated. Her students try not to appear too interested, but she can see most of them are at least somewhat intrigued by the unique photographs of doors on display.

Claire slows down her speech and intentionally looks at each of her students while explaining about their new project. She tries to speak to them as if they're just having a conversation together rather than listening to a teacher's lecture. "During this period, I would like each of you to get up and examine these pictures of distinct doors carefully but focus on what you can imagine is going on behind these doors. After you have had an opportunity to study each one of them, I want you to choose the door that best represents your particular story. If more than one of you choose the same door, that is not a problem. I will just run more copies."

Before she tells them to get up, Claire removes one of the photos from the wall. At first, she holds it vertically like a typical door would hang but then slowly lays it across the palm of her right hand in front of the students. She turns the photo over slowly with her left hand as if she's opening up a book. "Once you open your door, what story do you see behind it? Is what happens on the other side of your door fiction, nonfiction, fantasy, mystery, comedy, or tragedy? This is going to be your tale to tell, so it can be whatever you would like your narrative to be."

Claire gestures for her students to get up and walk around the room to check out the photographs while she continues, "Do any of these doors trigger a memory or call out to you for another reason? Do any of these doors appeal to you solely because of their appearance and style, or do they evoke a time or a place? Do any of these doors recall your past or suggest your future? What story do you wish to tell? What happens behind the door you have chosen? What is your story? What is hidden behind your door?"

As Claire walks around the classroom, she purposely repeats herself over and over to make sure her students really think about what they want to say but more importantly what they *need* to say. She wishes she could come right out and ask them to tell her what is wrong but knows that would not be advisable. Claire needs them to decide for themselves whether or not to tell their story on their own terms.

She notices several students appear as though they have already decided. "If you know which door you want, you may remove it from the clip and take it back to your seat." Within the first fifteen minutes, all but three of her sixteen students return to their desk with their chosen door. Claire approaches the remaining three and asks, "May I help you with your decision, or do you have any questions?"

"Are we allowed to take more than one door?" two of the students inquire.

"Of course. Just let me know if I need to run any copies for you." Claire waits for the third student to say something, but he just continues to look at the remaining photographs for a few more minutes before hesitantly removing the photograph of the high school's clear glass doors and promptly returning to his seat.

"Is everyone pleased with their choice or choices since a couple of you took more than one?" she eagerly asks her students and watches them all nod with their satisfaction.

"All right then. I want you to spend the next few days working on your story during this period—for homework if necessary—and not just a few sentences please. Make sure it is more like an entire chapter or as lengthy as a short story. By Friday, I want all the spelling and grammar checked before you turn your story into me—either electronically, printed, or both. If I feel it has not been written to the best of your ability, I will give it back to you to work on over the weekend. You all have access to computers and laptops at school if you don't have one at home. The school laptops can also be checked out with my written permission." Claire acknowledges a couple of her students who wish to check out laptops supplied by the school, so she quickly fills out the requested forms and hands them out to the two of them.

"This is extremely important, so listen up please. For this 'Behind the Door' project, the title of your story will be the name you give to your door." She pulls down one of the leftover photographs off the wall of a tiny, child-sized door and suggests, "You may wish to call it the 'Behind the *Down the Rabbit Hole* Door,' for example." She lays that one down and then removes another. For the medieval-looking door Claire selected, she proposes, "This one could be called the 'Behind the *Dungeons and Dragons* Door' or 'Behind the *Mid-evil* Door,' spelled in a different way." She writes the homophones *Mid-evil* and *Medieval* on the whiteboard for them to see the previous play on words. "Use your homonyms, synonyms, and puns. Be creative with your titles but try to capture the essence of your story in your title.

"All of you know why you are in this class. You are all gifted, talented, intelligent individuals, but you're here because you are not living up to your potential and have closed yourself off from the outside world. You might have similar explanations or a completely different reason than the student seated next to you, but all sixteen of you have one thing in common. You are all keeping something buried deep inside of you that is preventing you from living your life to your fullest potential. Because of my previous career as a group therapist, I know for a fact that it is much easier to face things as a group rather than as an individual. This is your chance to share your story. This is the time to use your voice. No one here will judge you. It's time for you to unlock your door and tell your story. What have you been hiding behind your door? What story do you need to tell? What happened behind your door?"

Claire carefully watches her students' reactions when she makes her next announcement. "Next week, you will all have the opportunity to read your story in front of the class. We will draw names each day to see who will be heard during that period. Remember, you all agreed that everything divulged within this classroom stays confidential within this group." A few of the sixteen cringe at the thought of reading theirs out loud, but no one verbally voices their complaints or objections.

While her students begin their outlines or jot down a few thoughts, Claire moves around the room and writes down which door or doors each of them had chosen. She pulls out her list of the students' choices to compare her guesses with their actual selections. Claire is surprised how few of them she actually matched and wonders if she even knows her students at all after spending the last couple of months working with this special class of sixteen.

Chapter 3

On her way to work Thursday morning, she receives a text message from each of her sons within minutes of each other, both inquiring how she's doing. Claire was hoping to make it through her workday before dwelling on the fact that today would have been her and her husband's fortieth wedding anniversary. She waits until she has parked her car at school before responding via text to both of them. "I'm doing fine. Happy heavenly fortieth anniversary, Peter. I miss your dad too. Thank you both for checking on me, but no need to be concerned. Love you both."

She stays in her car and waits for Paul and Chase to reply with some sort of emoji or sticker, and neither one of them disappoints her. She quickly grabs her laptop, tote bag, and purse and makes her way into the high school and then directly to her first-floor classroom at the end of the hall.

As her students file inside after the first bell, Claire receives her first five submissions for the "Behind the Door" project—both online and printed versions for each. She's surprised and elated to see those same five students immediately take their seats and quietly take out their study materials for other classes.

While the rest of the students finish working on their "Behind the Door" stories during class, she opens up her laptop to start reading one of the completed works she's received. After reading only the first two pages, Claire has a gnawing pit in her stomach and tears in her eyes. Emotionally, she cannot continue—especially today—and quickly closes her laptop. She inconspicuously gazes up to make sure none of her students have noticed her crying and is relieved to see all sixteen remain busy working at their desks.

Claire knows these teenagers need to open up, and that is precisely why she designed this project for them; however, if all of the submissions are as devastating and intimate as the first one she attempted to read, she begins questioning whether or not they should even be read aloud in front of their class of peers. Even though Claire is not one hundred percent sure if what she had read actually happened, it fits perfectly with the student's profile and behavior.

By the time the first period is over, Claire has received all but four of her students' stories. As the class begins to file out, she reminds the others to turn their projects in before the end of their class tomorrow. Claire packs up her laptop, her purse, and her large leather tote bag and heads to the counselor's office where she will be filling in once again this week until one o'clock.

While covering the counselor's position for the third time this week, quite a few students stop by to speak with her about their college choices or credits needed before graduation, and even several of them report bullying incidents on behalf of other students or to discuss their own peer-pressure situations.

Right as she's packing up to leave for the day, a frightened young freshman girl rushes in and quickly shuts the door. It's quite apparent she had been crying for quite some time, so Claire offers her several tissues to wipe her eyes. The girl tries to whisper, but the volume of her voice escalates through her terrified cries. "I think I'm pregnant," she hysterically blurts out.

Even though it's against the district rules to touch or hug a student, Claire quickly goes over to her and wraps her arms around her to help settle her down. She gently rocks her back and forth for several minutes trying to comfort her before asking, "Have you taken a pregnancy test?"

She blubbers her response, "No, but I'm late."

"So you've had intercourse with someone within the past few months?"

"No, but he touched me down there with his—" The distraught young girl is too immature and embarrassed to even mention the word *penis* out loud.

Claire tries again to ascertain the situation. "But he never actually inserted his penis inside of you at all?"

"No," the student timidly, but adamantly, responds. "I refused to take off my underwear."

"Well, then, I don't see how you could possibly be pregnant," Claire informs her while giving her a comforting smile.

The young student looks guardedly relieved and tries to return the smile.

"Let me get you something to read that should ease your mind." She finds the brochures about teenage sex and one explaining both the male and female anatomy and hands them to her. Claire shows her several illustrations and points out a section thoroughly explaining how everything works during sex. "It would be to your benefit to read these over very carefully and ask a trustworthy adult if you have any questions."

The student discretely puts the literature into an inside zippered pocket of her backpack. Claire waits until she gets her attention back before adding, "There are several medical reasons for having a late period, so if you continue to be late, you should contact your doctor, and don't be in such a rush to start having sex. You are far too young to even consider it."

She watches as the relieved student rushes out of the counselor's office as quickly as she had entered. Claire goes over the past few hours in her mind: *bullying, peer pressure, sex, teen pregnancy, drugs and alcohol, stress of college or not getting in at all, and parental and student expectations.* She can't even imagine what other issues might be uncovered through her own students' writings.

At the end of her counselor shift, she heads down the hallway toward the faculty parking lot. Claire is stunned when she notices one of her first-period students walking with several of his former friends, smiling and even chuckling as she observes him.

He waves and gives a genuinely friendly acknowledgment toward her as he passes by, "Hey, Dr. Claire."

She's so dumbfounded; all she can do is smile and wave back. Claire is not sure what to make of this miraculous change in him but is delighted to finally see him happy with his head held high. She hopes it has something to do with writing down his story, but only time will tell.

By the time she reaches her car, she has already decided to put off running the errands she had originally scheduled for today. She's too eager to get home to start reading her students' stories in the privacy of her own home.

Chapter 4

While pouring herself an iced tea, Claire remembers to retrieve a box of tissues before she opens up her laptop to restart the first story—one of the submissions including two different doors.

The first picture is a nondescript, unfinished flat-panel wooden door. It is entitled "Behind the *Grin and Bare It* Door" by Emily S.

> I will never forget my fourteenth birthday. It was the first day the upperclassman I had such a huge crush on smiled at me as we were leaving school. When he found out it was my birthday, I was shocked when he walked over to me and leaned down to give me a tender kiss on the cheek.
>
> "Happy Birthday, Emily," he whispered as he started to walk away, but then he stopped and softly shouted back to me. "Are you doing anything special to celebrate?"
>
> All I could do was shake my head in response because I was still trying to process the fact that he actually knew my name. When he started walking back toward me, I thought I was going to pass out because my heart was beating so fast.
>
> "How about if I meet you under the bleachers around eight o'clock tonight? We can celebrate together." He didn't even wait for my answer because he knew without a doubt I would be there.

My entire body was trembling on my way home from school that day. "He couldn't possibly feel the same way about me that I felt about him, could he?" I asked myself over and over, trying to justify his actions. "He's three years older than me, a jock, and can get any girl he wants. His parents are filthy rich and even gave him a brand-new car for his sixteenth birthday. What could he possibly want with a middle-class, flat-chested, and scrawny nerd like me?"

I can't even recall what excuse I gave my teetotaler, church-abiding parents for going out that evening or whether I even gave them one at all. My mind was clearly on more important things—like him.

His favorite color was blue, so I put on my prettiest blue dress, and I knew he usually dated girls with long wavy hair, so I even curled my long hair and fastened it to one side with a blue barrette. Normally I wouldn't use a purse, but I did that night to hold the makeup I wanted to put on after I left the house. My parents never would have allowed me to wear any, and I even thought to bring a makeup remover wipe with me so I could remove the evidence before I returned home.

Shortly after seven, I carefully climbed onto my bicycle and rode to the football field. I hid my bike next to the maintenance shed quite a ways away so I wouldn't look like such an immature child. After putting on my makeup, I hurriedly walked the rest of the long way across the field and then all the way around behind the bleachers to the center section.

It seemed like an eternity waiting for him to join me, but once I saw him approaching, I questioned what I was even thinking. "What was I doing there? What was I doing there with him?" I nervously asked myself.

When he got within a few feet of me, he quickly turned his back to me, and my first thought was that he changed his mind and was leaving until I heard the flick of his lighter and saw the dancing light emanating from a flame. He turned back around and was holding a professionally decorated cupcake with a lit birthday candle on top.

"Make a wish, birthday girl," he told me in a strange, unsettling tone. As soon as I blew out the candle, he set the cupcake down on one of the bleachers and started feverishly kissing and touching me. I could instantly smell and taste the liquor on his breath, and I kept thinking he was acting so zealously because he had been drinking. Who was I to stop my big crush from kissing and touching me on my birthday? We were just making out under the bleachers like countless other students had done over the years, and I fell prey to his intoxicated advances.

I remember chuckling to myself when he pulled a bottle of 7Up out of his back pocket for me to drink. He put it down on one of the bleacher seats to open it for me. "A toast to your birthday, Emily. I didn't think you would want any liquor," he said while handing me the 7Up bottle. He then pulls out a beer for himself from his other pocket. "Cheers," he toasts after clinking our two bottles together.

After a few sips of my soft drink, I could instantly feel my senses escaping me. My body folded to the ground as if my bones had suddenly vanished. I tried to tell him something was wrong with me, but I couldn't utter a sound. Before losing all my faculties, I remembered feeling confused watching him just standing over me, laughing at my dilemma.

I can only recall flashes of him raping me on the filthy ground beneath the stadium bleachers. He was so proud of himself for taking away my virginity and devilishly laughed at me for thinking he would want anything else from me other than his sexual conquest. He kept slapping me across the face and telling me to stay with him or to open my eyes so I could watch as he smeared my virginal blood and his sperm all over the front of my beautiful blue dress before raping me again. I felt like a ragdoll—the way he easily tossed me about.

I'm not quite sure how many times he assaulted me that night. I lost count after what I believe was the fifth time within what seemed like an hour or two and was grateful to slip into unconsciousness before he also conquered my remaining orifices.

It was still dark out when I finally came to. My face was covered with his fluids and my blood, and both were starting to dry on my skin. When I tried to sit up, the pain I felt was a shocking realization of the evening's previous events. I crawled over to the lower bleachers so I could get some leverage to pull myself up to a standing position because my legs were still violently shaking. My only thought at that point was to get home and out of sight before the sun came up. I could see my purse tossed under one of the bleachers, but there was no way I was going to be able to retrieve it in my current condition.

It took me forever to cross the football field with the agonizing pain I was experiencing, but it was nothing compared to the excruciating pain I felt while riding my bicycle home. As much as I wanted to quit riding it, I knew if I didn't use it, I would not reach my house in time.

I hid my bike behind the garage so I could clean the blood stains off the seat before school in just a few hours. Thankfully, the house key was still in its hiding place, and I managed to crawl up to the second-floor bathroom without waking up my parents on the first floor. I knew I couldn't clean myself up with any terry-cloth towels, so I used toilet paper for my body and quietly soaked my dress until I could work on it at a later time. Until then, I hadn't even noticed I was no longer wearing any underpants. My first thought was that he must have taken them as a trophy for his conquest, plus he must have removed both bottles and the cupcake as well. I was the only remaining evidence of his heinous, abusive acts.

When I heard my bedroom alarm go off, I bit my lips together while trying to run into my bedroom to turn it off before my parents got suspicious. I immediately returned to the bathroom and stood under the shower scrubbing myself with soap from head to toe as if trying to wash away any memory of my fourteenth birthday. I was too ashamed to tell anyone how stupid and gullible I had been, but I should have.

When he walked past me in the school hallway the following day, I moved off to the side and refused to look up at him. Without anyone noticing, he stepped over close to me and whispered, "Thanks for last night and the lovely panties."

The second picture is a door with three horizontal bubble-glass panes inserted into a dark cherry-red painted door. It is entitled "Behind the *Pains Beyond the Panes* Door" by Emily S.

> I was almost two months along in my pregnancy before his family acknowledged me. He and his father were both in denial until his mother found several pairs of blood and semen-stained underpants in between his mattress and box spring and a couple more in the glovebox of his car. She wouldn't have even looked through his things if I hadn't mentioned that I believed her son took mine for a trophy after taking my virginity and raping me multiple times on my fourteenth birthday.
>
> My parents still have no idea that I was raped and got pregnant that night, but I know they would somehow blame me and disown me for what happened. Everything about that night was against their religion and strict beliefs, and I didn't want the additional pain of losing them too.
>
> My rapist's mother sincerely tried to be kind to me. She gave me the choice of keeping the baby with the financial assistance of his family, without any accountability from him or his father of course, or giving my baby up for adoption or having an abortion. She would be there for me—whatever I decided.
>
> To me, there was no choice. I loathed having anything of his inside of me and wanted it removed as soon as possible. I couldn't imagine loving his child conceived in that way. The child would be a constant reminder of the worst night of my life.

His mother drove me to the clinic with the red door and three horizontal glass-door inserts two counties away. She paid for all the expenses with cash and then drove me back home once the doctor said it was medically safe to do so.

I actually felt sorry for her handling her son's mistake on her own, knowing that he had also raped quite a few other virgins besides me. She had to pull the car over several times on the drive home so she could run around to the shoulder to vomit. I even drove for a few miles because at one point she was sobbing so uncontrollably, I knew she could no longer see the road.

His mother and I barely look at each other now if we accidentally cross paths in public, but every month, the two of us meet at a remote location just to check on each other. She was relieved to tell me her son is now on drugs to control his hypersexuality and he's seeing a therapist about his compulsive sexual behavior. She knows he should be behind bars for what he has already done, but as his mother, she just can't find it in her heart to turn him in to the authorities—and neither can I.

I know it's a really twisted relationship caring so much about my rapist's mother and for her to care so much about one of her son's victims, but somehow, we've formed a very close bond. We love and need each other because it's easier than going through this shameful secret all alone.

Claire closes her laptop and grabs another tissue. She aimlessly walks around several rooms trying to comprehend and digest Emily's story believing it to be the truth. She prays that the other submissions will not be so intense. On the other hand, as a therapist, Claire is extremely proud of Emily for opening up and telling her life-changing story. After a necessary short break, Claire gets back to reading the submissions.

The next is a picture of a gunmetal door with twelve raised panels but no inset windows. It is entitled "Behind the *Camouflaged Quandary* Door" by Brad E.

> My dad only had three weeks left of his second tour when the two uniformed officers knocked on our front door. They were there to inform us he had been killed in action. I was only nine years old at the time, but I fully understood why everyone walked on eggshells around me and whispered with pity as soon as I entered the room.
>
> My mom was my rock and my best friend back then. We depended on each other when my dad was away on tour, and that didn't change after he died. For a time, it even brought us closer. She never wanted me to feel like I was missing out on anything even though I didn't have a dad anymore. If he had promised to help me with fielding a ball when he got back, she was there to hit baseballs to me at the local diamond. If I missed going fishing with my dad, she was in the boat baiting a hook right alongside me. Even throughout cub scouts, my mom was helping out as a den mother for as long as she could.
>
> She finally had to go back to work to help out with expenses, but I always saw her for breakfast before she left and then again once she returned home.
>
> I could talk to her about anything because she was truly my best friend. Don't get me wrong. I hung around the neighborhood kids during the summer and classmates throughout the school year, but I couldn't wait until it was dinnertime,

so I had a legitimate excuse to go home to be with my mom.

It was more than two years after my dad died before I started seeing a real change in her personality. She had always had a glass or two of wine with dinner even when my dad was still alive, but now she was having one before dinner, a couple during, and several more afterward. She started buying more pre-packaged frozen dinners or canned meals and rarely cooked for us anymore. We didn't have our mealtime together or our bedtime talks anymore. We didn't even give each other a hug and kiss goodbye, and laughter was just another forgotten thing from my past.

Because of her excessive drinking, Mom started missing too many days at work. When she did make it into her job, she was an hour late because she was too hungover from the night before to wake up and get ready on time. Her boss tried several times to get her help with her alcohol addiction, but she never even made it through the second step of the twelve-step program.

The day she showed up drunk to work, wearing her nightgown, was the day he was forced to let her go. I was so embarrassed that day when her former boss carried her passed-out body over his shoulder and into our house while my friends were walking by after our baseball practice. Everyone could see that she wasn't even wearing any underwear, and I was so angry with her for humiliating me that day. When her ex-boss was leaving, he blatantly told me I would be better off living in a foster home.

Even though I had just turned twelve, that was the day I took over running our household.

I sorted through all the bills she had just stashed into the kitchen drawers because she didn't want to be bothered with paying them. Every single one was a final notice, but I called each of the companies to set up a payment plan, which they reluctantly agreed to do but only because I lied and said my mother's illness was a temporary setback and she was already getting better. I also played the pity card since Dad had died protecting our country, but I was desperate.

Without my mom's paycheck, the money we got from the government wouldn't cover all of our bills with the late fees and interest payments, so I started working two jobs to help pay down our debt; however, I absolutely refused to pay for my mother's booze.

Seven days a week I would be up by three o'clock in the morning to roll up newspapers and stuff them with their advertising inserts. I had to deliver them using my undersized bicycle until the snow got too deep, and then I would have to walk my entire route. Late afternoons, I either mowed lawns or shoveled sidewalks and driveways depending on the season and the weather. On occasion, there would be bonus work like cleaning out a garage, raking leaves, or fixing a fence—especially during school breaks.

Almost a year ago, I rushed home from school so I could get to the bank before it closed for the Thanksgiving holiday. I needed to deposit my earnings from my previous month's work in order to pay our bills that were due the following week. I was devastated when I entered the house and saw everything had been tossed around as if a tornado had ripped through every room in our house.

When I got upstairs to make sure my cash was still hidden, I saw my mother passed out on the floor next to her bed—still holding onto a nearly empty bottle of liquor. I didn't even have to confirm the fact that she had found my money and used it to buy more liquor.

Without thinking more about it, I wrote a note and signed it with my mother's signature allowing me to pawn my dad's purple heart so I could pay our bills due the following week. I contacted the liquor store and advised them never to bring another bottle to our house again because if they did, I would tell the police they were delivering it to me—a minor. It was somewhat comical to hear she always paid her debt to them in cash at the time of their delivery because she had never set up an account with them.

When I started picking up the house after her rampage, I was devastated and heartbroken when I picked up the sofa cushions and saw my father's ashes flung all over the living room carpet and fireplace hearth. She had broken the seal on the urn and shook the contents out to see if that was where I hid my money and then just tossed it aside as if it didn't mean anything to her. I tried to retrieve my father's ashes, but they just sunk deeper into the carpeting. The only ones I managed to return to the urn were the ashes still laying on the brick hearth.

First it was her theft of all my money I had worked so hard for, then it was having to pawn my father's purple heart to pay our bills, and finally her total disregard for my father's remains. I completely lost it. At that point, I didn't care if she lived or died because I knew I was better off without her, but I also didn't care if I lived or died. I was so exhausted from years of being deprived of love, sleep, and food to the stress of taking care of everything on my own to watching my mother slowly killing herself with alcohol. I closed my eyes and prayed God would take me so I could be with my father instead.

Our neighbors called for a wellness check on our house four days later. My mother and I were rushed to the hospital, and everyone thought we had been assaulted because our house had been vandalized by an outsider. I chose not to correct them because the simple truth was I still loved my mother and didn't want her to be called an unfit mother and I did not want to go into foster care. Deep down I knew that all of her problems began just because she couldn't cope with the death of her husband—my father. That wasn't her fault.

When they brought us home from the hospital a few days later, we were both shocked to see our entire house had been picked up and cleaned by all the neighbors. They had stocked our refrigerator and left casseroles packed for us in the freezer as well. I couldn't help but break down and sob when I realized the rest of my father's ashes were simply vacuumed away and thrown out with the rest of the garbage and I didn't even have his purple heart for a remembrance anymore.

One of the neighbors from down the street stopped by and told me to follow him upstairs. He opened up my bedroom closet and moved a box aside on my upper shelf to reveal several expensive bottles full of liquor. "I thought you could hide these from your mother, but I didn't want to dump out the liquor because you could sell the sealed bottles back to the liquor store if you need a little extra cash." He then opened up my top dresser drawer and pulled out the case with my father's purple heart inside. "The guy at the pawnshop and I are old buddies from the service. He contacted me the day you brought it in. We took up a collection from other servicemen in the area to buy it back from him, and the leftover cash we collected is stashed under your T-shirts. I know your house wasn't broken into, son. It was your mother's doing, wasn't it?"

I was afraid to answer him even though I was so grateful for everything he had done for me—for us. All I could do was continue to cry.

He handed me a piece of notepaper with his name and phone number written on it. "Call me if you ever need help with your mother. I'm a recovering alcoholic, and she would be more than welcome to join me for our AA meetings."

The next few days were wonderful. My mom was actually sober for the first time in years. We laughed again and cooked dinner together and had a difficult discussion about the effect alcohol has had on both of our lives and how sorry she was to have caused me such pain and hardship for all those years.

Because I hadn't shown up for my newspaper delivery job for a few days and hadn't called them to be excused during my absence, they gave my job to someone else. It turned out to be a blessing because I ended up getting a job after school and on every other weekend for less hours and at twice the salary.

My mother fixed me breakfast before school, but I knew something was wrong because she barely touched her plate. I told her how proud of her I was and how much I loved her, but it wasn't enough. While I was attending school, she left that morning before the dishes were even done. All we had were just those few days of normalcy before she pawned both of their wedding rings and abandoned me.

I never reported it because I knew I would end up in foster care. I had already lost both of my parents, and I didn't want to lose my home too. I've been doing pretty well living on my own ever since. I have lots of experience because I've been taking care of myself since I was twelve years old.

Claire feels so sorry for Brad but can understand his desire to continue taking care of himself. Ever since she has known him, she always felt he was older than his years and was impressed by his maturity, ambition, and determination. She's also glad she doesn't have to report him because she feels he is right where he belongs at the present time, but she will discuss foster care with him sometime in the near future, especially when loneliness wains on him. Finding the right foster parents for a teenager can be very difficult, but she wants him to have a somewhat normal family life while he is still so young.

Before picking up the next student's story, Claire even considers fostering Brad herself but realizes that would be impossible considering her age. She decides to try to figure out some other way to help him, but for now, she has only gotten through a couple assignments and needs to move on to Erika's tale.

The next picture has old, weathered arched church doors with stained-glass panel insets above. The story is entitled "Behind the *Hell on Earth* Door" by Erika B.

Each time I go to the cemetery to visit my twin brother, Ethan, I pass by these familiar, old church doors coming and going. The church was where Ethan and I had been both baptized and confirmed, and now he is buried in the cemetery adjacent to the church.

Every Sunday I go through these doors to attend weekly church services with my mom and dad, but I dread stepping inside now because all I can see is my brother's funeral with the closed casket parked at the front of the altar and his framed picture staring back at me. It had once been a portrait of the two of us, but my mom took a scissor to it and discarded my half in the trash.

For the past couple of years, going to church on Sunday has become a weekly reminder to my parents that they lost their favorite child—their precious son, Ethan. They enter through these church doors pretending to be loving, happy, and respectful but always exit sad, angry, and resentful.

After the church service, the three of us would walk over to Ethan's gravesite so they could say a few prayers, shed a few tears, and sometimes leave flowers or balloons on special occasions. At least he gets something from our parents on our shared birthday. I am completely overlooked now for birthdays and Christmas, even though it doesn't really matter. My past gifts from them were never as nice, thoughtful, or expensive as Ethan's. I was like an afterthought.

On the drive home from the church and the cemetery, they would both cry for him and scold me for not being more like their perfect, beautiful, loving son who is now an angel in heaven with God.

After six months, I couldn't take it anymore, so now I always walk the two miles home from church—even through blizzards if necessary—

rather than put up with their verbal abuse in the car. I should have told them the truth about their precious Ethan when it happened and even long before that, but he was my twin brother and my best friend, and I always tried to protect him.

Even if I had told them the truth, my parents wouldn't have believed me. Ethan could do no wrong in their eyes. He was super popular in school, but I didn't have many friends. He was a phenomenal football and baseball player and would definitely get an athletic scholarship for college, whereas I would prefer to be a spectator, and my grades were decent, but didn't warrant any grant money. He always went overboard being affectionate toward our parents even though he never meant it. I didn't bother showing our mom and dad much affection because I knew it wouldn't be reciprocated.

I first noticed his fearless tendencies in grade school when Ethan would do extremely daring stunts to show off for his classmates. The more dangerous the stunt, the better the show. He would climb the tallest trees he could find with absolutely no fear of falling. Several times he jumped from one branch to another while descending. Whenever he could find enough materials and a vacant lot, Ethan would build ramps to jump from one to the other with his bicycle and eventually jumped them with his small motorcycle. Even jumping over raging bonfires became too easy and not nearly dangerous enough to appease him.

But what scared me most of all was when he started tempting fate even without an audience to egg him on. I remember screaming at the top of my lungs for him to stop the day he stood in the middle of the train tracks and didn't jump off until a split second before the whistle-blowing freight train speedily passed. It seemed like an eternity waiting on the other side of the tracks for the boxcars to clear before I could make sure my brother had jumped off in time and was still alive.

Ethan's dangerous feats escalated rapidly. He got such a rush from them but always felt the need to take on even riskier challenges. He would watch extreme sports, daredevil, and superhero shows on his computer, laptop, or phone every chance he got and loved playing the videos repeatedly of insane stunts gone wrong where people had even lost their lives attempting them. Those death-defying stunts became his bucket list. He believed he was better than all of those who had failed and knew he would survive. Ethan couldn't wait to get his driver's license so he could advance his speed and jump using a car or a full-size motorcycle. Nothing could hurt him when he was on his adrenaline high because Ethan believed he was invincible.

Dad was still at work, and Mom had run to the store because we were out of Ethan's favorite cereal and shampoo. My brother kept egging me on to watch the videos of some of the stunts that had gone terribly wrong, but I refused. He kept laughing and shouting at the stunt people and daredevils who were severely hurt or killed, calling them *idiots* and *morons*. I finally got so frustrated with him that I climbed out onto the flat roof outside of my bedroom window where I would go when I wanted to get away from him or our parents.

He kept calling out my name, but I refused to answer him. I could hear him jiggling the doorknob on my bedroom door, but it was locked. Ethan kept begging for me to answer the door to let him in until I finally gave in and opened it before he broke it down and blamed me somehow.

Ethan was so excited to gain access to the flat roof extending from my bedroom. "I want to show you something, sis," he said as he jumped out my window onto the flat roof. I was still inside my bedroom when I heard him yell, "Watch this!" I was horrified when I looked back at him just as he was attempting to do a backward swan dive off of the flat section of the roof. I'm not sure if it was because of our connection as twins, but I actually felt him hit the ground, and it knocked the breath right out of me the instant I sensed he had died.

I prayed I was wrong and ran down the stairs and out the back door to see if he was still alive, but his mangled body confirmed he wasn't. I frantically called 911 anyway even though I knew deep down there was nothing they could do to revive him.

The paramedics arrived a couple of minutes before my mom returned. They all assumed Ethan broke his legs, arms, back, and neck after he accidentally fell off of my flat roof. I didn't tell them otherwise, even after our parents told me his death was probably my fault. It was my flat roof he fell from, and he wouldn't have even been out there if it wasn't to join me out there. At one point, my father even insinuated I might have pushed him because of my jealousy toward Ethan. I haven't spoken a word to my father

> since his accusation. By both of their actions and words, I know they wish it had been me instead of their precious, perfect son.
>
> I hope Ethan appreciates all the suffering I am going through keeping his secrets from our parents. I didn't just lose my twin brother that day. I also lost any chance of a parental connection with my mom and dad.

"Unbelievable," Claire says to herself. "How do I help them when they don't even have a parent at home to talk to for comfort or guidance?" She looks frustrated knowing that even though her students are finally opening up through their personal stories, she still may not be able to help them deal with everything. Claire is so overwhelmed reading their heartbreaking stories, she begins questioning herself and her "Behind the Door" project. How is she supposed to support and help her students who are dealing with such tragedies and chaos in their lives?

Chapter 5

After retrieving her mail and watering her planted herbs shelved within her kitchen bay window, Claire takes a quick bathroom break before refilling her drink and continuing on with her students' stories. Just seeing that the next assignment was written by Janine already has Claire on edge. In all the years she has known her, Claire has never seen Janine socialize with anyone—ever. She readies herself for a depressing read, knowing how lonely this student must be feeling on a daily basis.

The picture Janine chose is a straight, featureless door with a nearly invisible handle. It is entitled "Behind the *Cyberian Masquerade* Door" by Janine M.

> Since the first day we picked him up from the pound, my best friend has been my Siberian husky named Blue. I used to hang around with a few other girls in grade school but usually only during school hours. The only sleepover I was ever invited to ended with me going home early after they teased me about my out-of-style outfit and my childish dated pajamas. After that, it was easier just being by myself during lunch and study hall. Plus, I knew Blue would be at home to greet me when I returned after school.
>
> The older I got, the more I craved having a social life. It was great hanging around with Blue, but I needed to have more than a one-way conversation with a dog. That's when I started going

into chat rooms online. It was safe because there was no video or audio—just words typed out on a keyboard. I didn't have to worry about what I was wearing or how I looked or even how old I was. I could be whoever I wanted to be, and so could the person speaking with me. I even used a fake name and set up a special email account so no one could find out who I really was.

It was somewhat exciting not knowing the person on the other end. I could imagine them being my age, extremely popular, good-looking, and totally into me even though the exact opposite was probably true. Blue would always try to play ball with me while I was in the chat rooms, but that was okay because I didn't have a time restraint to respond to my Internet friends.

Sometimes, our cyber conversations would be very generic, talking about likes and dislikes, places we'd like to travel to, and favorite things, but after chatting with the same person over time, the subject always turned to either having a video chat or talking about sex. I would have to quit speaking with that person as soon as that would happen. I was still so young and naive. If they found out I wasn't even a teenager yet, I knew I would be locked out of the chat room for good.

My life consisted of attending school and spending time with Blue, and the rest of my time was spent online. My dad was a truck driver and was gone at least five days a week, and my mom worked the second shift at the local hospital, so I knew they would never catch me doing anything wrong during my social connections. By the time I hit my early teens, I could pass for someone much older because I was inherently big chested.

All my usual chat rooms had started video conversations, and I still craved the two-way conversations, so I needed to adapt even though I still wanted and needed to hide my identity. I found a Mardi Gras mask at the thrift store and also purchased a few tops to show off my cleavage and the size of my breasts so I could pass for at least eighteen years of age. I removed anything from my bedroom that might give away my true age and even practiced speaking in an older, sultry sounding voice.

The first time I entered the video chat room, I realized every male option available was at least in their mid-thirties to late fifties, but I was so desperate for someone to talk to that it didn't really matter to me.

Forty-two-year-old Kevin was my first choice because he posted where he lived and it was pretty far away from my location—if he hadn't lied. He wasn't very attractive, somewhat homely in fact, and a tad overweight, but he had kind eyes, and I thought we might have a lot in common because he seemed just as socially inept as I was. We talked for weeks every day when I supposedly got home from *work* even though it was actually getting home from *school*. Hiding behind the mask, I found it really easy to talk to him. I didn't know if he was telling me the truth either, but it really didn't matter. We were just cyber friends.

After the first month, he started bringing up the subject of sex. I was still a virgin, but I had done quite a bit of reading on the subject, so I could play along within the conversation. He loved that I was wearing a mask because it just made me appear more mysterious, which he thought was very sexy. Kevin finally got bold enough to ask if he could see my breasts. At first, I was surprised by his request, but I was so worried about losing Kevin as my cyber friend, I complied by lifting up my top while still wearing my bra. I was grateful that he was satisfied with the partial reveal for the time being.

Every day we both got a little bolder in our requests, our language, and our compliance. I couldn't wait to get home from school so I could spend time with Kevin. But I also realized he wasn't really enough to satisfy me, so I told him my work schedule had changed and I would only be able to spend Monday, Wednesday, and Friday nights with him from now on. He was visibly upset but went along with it because I wasn't dropping him completely.

Bradon became my next cyber friend. He was in his thirties and seemed to be more sociable and was much better looking than Kevin. I would be with him on Tuesdays, Thursdays, and Saturdays when possible. But Bradon kept encouraging me to reveal myself. He didn't like my Mardi Gras mask and wanted to see my face. After we had spent several months together, I decided to put on a bunch of makeup to look older, and I removed my mask for him. He kept telling me how beautiful I was and that I shouldn't hide behind the mask ever again, plus I should use less makeup.

The next time we were going to be together, I decided to appear as myself to see what would happen. I raced home from school to show Bradon the real me, but there was my mom, standing in the kitchen, just smiling at me. The hospital had finally granted her request and changed her hours, so she was now on the first shift and would be able to be home to spend time with me from dinnertime to bedtime.

My first thought was how could she do that to me? She's taking away my time with my friends. What am I going to do now? I needed to get on the Internet as soon as possible.

I made up an excuse that I had lots of homework and went upstairs to my bedroom to contact Bradon. He was somewhat surprised but I think a little turned on to the fact that I was much younger than I had been pretending. I explained my situation, but he just said he would be there for me whenever I was available.

I didn't remove my mask for Kevin, but I did tell him how old I was. I was devastated when he blocked me the following day, but it was just as well because my mom's new schedule was going to cut into my cyber social life as it was.

Every chance I got during school, I would contact Bradon. Even during some of my classes, I would sit in the back of the room and chat with him on my laptop for as long as I could. He worked from home, so my staggered schedule didn't seem to bother him. When we couldn't speak out loud to each other, we typed out our words to each other instead. I loved watching him when he had to get up from his desk to retrieve something because he was always wearing just his T-shirt and very revealing tight briefs.

Mom was busy making dinner because my dad would be returning home that night. I went upstairs to work on my *homework* and tried to contact Bradon, but I couldn't get through. It wasn't like he had blocked me. It was more like his account had been frozen. I tried over and over again to get through, but it wouldn't work. I was in such a panic to connect with someone, I even tried Kevin, who I prayed had unblocked me. I was happily surprised when he accepted my request, but he was even more surprised seeing me without my Mardi Gras mask. He told me how much he had missed me and missed our conversations and was hoping I would try to contact him again. I offered to put the mask back on, but he said I shouldn't hide such a beautiful face and he would try very hard to accept the fact that I was so young and still in high school.

With no time to explain to Kevin, I quickly closed my laptop when my mom abruptly entered my bedroom and told me to come downstairs at once. She even waited for me in my doorway, and by the look on her face, I knew she was extremely upset.

As I descended the stairs, I could see a man and a woman both wearing dark suits standing in our living room. They introduced themselves to me, and as soon as I heard the words *sergeant*, *officer*, and *detectives*, I knew I was in some sort of trouble. My mom sat down on the couch with me as they sat across from us and explained they were investigating certain individuals who frequented several chat rooms online and knew I had been in contact with the male known as Bradon.

They asked me several questions before the male officer asked my mom to join him in another room. The female officer started asking me about any sexual conversations with Bradon: Were we involved with removing our clothing or performing sexual acts in front of each other? Had he ever asked me to meet him in person? Had he told me he loved me? Had he ever contacted me directly or was I the one to initiate our chats?

I answered her questions truthfully because I was too afraid not to. I assumed they had access to his account and knew some of our chats were actually typed out during the video sessions during school. Bradon had told me he wanted to meet me in person just that week. He would tell me he loved spending time with me but never told me directly that he loved me—only that he was starting to fall for me. And I felt so ashamed when I realized that I was the only one to initiate our chats. Bradon never contacted me first.

When she explained that Bradon had been arrested on three counts of rape and one count of attempted murder involving girls he was chatting with online, I couldn't accept it. She must be mistaken. My Bradon wouldn't hurt anyone. He was a gentle, kind, and a thoughtful young man and could not have done any of those criminal things.

The officer knew I was having a difficult time accepting what she was saying, so she brought out evidence to show me. First, she showed me his rap sheet listing petty crimes since he was a preteen and even a stint in prison in his twenties for an assault on a girlfriend. I could see the entries for the recent rapes and attempted murder, but I still didn't want to believe it.

The first photo she laid in front of me was a picture of the wall behind Bradon's desk and computer. There were seven blown-up screenshots of girls around my age displayed in a straight row. The second and fifth portraits had a slash through their faces. The officer explained that these were two of the girls he had raped. The sixth portrait with the check mark was the girl he had raped and believed he had murdered, but she had miraculously survived his attempt.

I asked what the sticky note was doing on my picture and the girl's picture next to me. The officer explained that we were targeted to be his next victims. Bradon had already purchased tickets for the two of us to fly to New Orleans because of the Mardi Gras mask I had first worn during our chats. He had already checked on remote houses to rent there during Mardi Gras and was planning on booking one as soon as I agreed to meet him for a few days. Bradon would always take his victims to locations relating to their previous chats. It became both his signature and his downfall because that is how they finally caught up with him.

My mom and the sergeant returned minutes before my dad got home. She stayed with me while the sergeant took my dad into the other room to explain what was going on. I could hear my dad wailing because of the difficult news, and I could tell my mom had been crying as well. I was still in denial, and all I wanted to do was get up to my computer in my bedroom to be with Kevin and my dog, Blue. It didn't even dawn on me that he would do anything wrong. I just knew he would listen to me because he was one of my best—and now my only—friend besides Blue.

Before they left, they confiscated my hard drive from my computer and took my laptop with them. I was so desperate to speak with Kevin I asked if I could use my laptop for a few minutes before they left. The sergeant privately informed me that Kevin was also being investigated by their team and I would be wise to socialize in person with classmates closer to my own age from school.

Needless to say, my Internet privileges were taken away, and I am still trying to cope with the loss. I did manage to contact Kevin by borrowing a classmate's laptop and explained why I wasn't going to be able to contact him again. He immediately disconnected.

When I got home from school that day, my parents informed me I was grounded for another month because they were informed I had entered a chat room without permission. Blue is now back to being my only friend again, but I truly miss my cyber connection with Kevin and Bradon. Even though I now know how dangerous cyber addiction can be, I still can't help but crave it because I desperately need someone *human* to connect with.

Oh, that's so sad and frightening, Claire thinks to herself. Unfortunately, this is not the first case she has come across regarding cyber addiction. She recalls the daughter of a friend of hers who ran off to meet her cyber friend, but thankfully she changed her mind minutes before getting off the train to meet him in the city. Her cyber friend was arrested the following week for a near-fatal assault of another girl.

As she gets up from her chair, Claire's stomach begins to remind her it is time to eat; however, instead of an entire meal, Claire fixes herself a light snack and then hurriedly returns to her laptop to read Dave's story. She's eager to find out why he was the last student to choose his door and especially curious to find out why he chose one so transparent.

The picture is a clear-glass double door from the main entry at the high school. It is entitled "Behind the *Nowhere to Hide* Door" by Dave T.

Until middle school, I always had plenty of friends in the neighborhood to play with after school and during the summer break. But when all of my friends started growing like weeds while going through puberty, I did not. Unfortunately, I stayed back in the twentieth percentile for growth for two more years in a row.

At first it was just name-calling like Shrimp, Shorty, or Tiny, but then the teasing became less verbal and more physical. The bullies always seemed to pick on the smaller ones because we weren't as strong or big enough to fight back. I didn't mind hanging out with the other non-growers in my class since we had something in common, but the physical attacks and verbal bullying became so much worse if we stayed together. It was their mission to torment us and keep us apart.

By the time I was a freshman, my growth percentile had increased tremendously, and I had either caught up to or surpassed my classmates; however, I was already branded as an easy target, and anyone who hung around with me became a target too.

It became so much easier just to be by myself. During lunch period, I would get permission to go to the school library to use the computer equipment, and after school, I would race home as fast as I could because I knew the bullies and popular kids always liked to hang around and socialize with each other for a while after school or were tied up with their team sports or extracurricular activities.

In between classes were my most difficult challenges. I could never keep my locker open long enough to put anything inside or take anything out. There was always someone there waiting to slam it shut. I lost count how many times I ended up with pinched or broken fingers or scrapes and bruising across the back of my hands from the force of the metal locker door against my skin.

Not a day went by when I wasn't threatened by someone who was going to hurt me if I didn't do something for them—whether it was giving them my money or doing their homework or performing an embarrassing act for their sadistic amusement. It was terrifying looking over my shoulder constantly from one period to another. The school hallways became battlegrounds, and I prayed every day I would not get permanently injured during the imminent conflict.

It was a little easier to function over the summer months. I would spend most of my time inside my house on the computer because I was still too exposed and vulnerable outside—even within my own yard, where I was used for target practice. I would go through deep depressions knowing my lot was cast, and I couldn't do anything to change it until I left for college where no one knew me. Every day I felt like I was unjustly imprisoned and locked up in solitary confinement.

One of the most frightening days of my life was when I was searching on the computer about depression in teenagers and stories about school shootings started popping up one right after the other. I started reading several of the shooter profiles online and realized it could have easily been my own bio I was reading: bullied, small in stature, unpopular, keeps to himself, inferior or lacking parental figures, depressed, angry, low self-esteem, access to weapons, bright but slacking student, or scared but resentful. I wondered what would put someone like me over the edge enough to kill innocent people for revenge or to have the *upper hand* just once in their life, and I was terrified of becoming that individual. What was their breaking point? What was *my* breaking point? How much more could I tolerate before I get pushed over the edge like these broken, unstable individuals who finally lost control?

I'm begging all of you—if you are one of the bullies, please consider what impact you are having on that person's life. If you aren't a bully but witness someone acting as one, please stop them before it's too late.

We have nowhere to hide here, but you won't either if we are finally pushed beyond our breaking point.

After reading his story, Claire now understands why it was so difficult for Dave to initially take the photo of the school door for his project story. Not only is he frightened by the ones who constantly bully and torment him, but he's also frightened of himself and his actions if he hits his own breaking point. Regrettably, there are countless numbers of bullied students just like Dave found in any school grade and even in the workplace.

Even though she had put protections in place for her sixteen students, as a therapist and as a school employee, she knows she cannot avoid reporting Dave to the authorities for their *watch list* of students who have all the red flags and the potential of becoming violent, but she also knows she can help Dave by getting him the professional counseling he needs to ensure he never reaches rock bottom or an uncontrollable urge to retaliate on his antagonizers as well as anyone else in his path. She's thankful Dave is well aware of her mandated reporting because the watch list was discussed during their first day of school and accepted by all of her *sixteen*.

Claire cries as she sadly fills out the watch list form online to report her student based on what he had written in his story. She prints off a copy of the filled-in form and throws it in an envelope along with several recommendations for counselors in the local area whom Dave should consider speaking with before it's too late. After she seals the envelope and addresses it to Dave, Claire desperately needs to get her mind off him for a while, so she wipes her eyes and picks up Elise's first-door story.

Elise's chosen first door is the paint-chipped broken door from the boarded-up house. It is entitled "Behind the *Before* Door" by Elise M.

> Before I could actually read the articles, I would thumb through my older sister's teen magazines and look at the pictures of all the new designer fashions and the beautiful female models with their perfect skinny figures, hair, and makeup. I would try to dress up my dolls to look just like them and tell myself I would look even better than the models and my sister when I got to be her age.
>
> I loved when she allowed me to sit on her bed to watch her get ready for a date. She would always take the time to put some lipstick on me or blush on my cheeks. My sister was always being chased by one boy or another mainly because of her good looks, but she was also very personable. She was extremely popular in school with both students and faculty members; however, my dream to become even more beautiful than her vanished into thin air years before I became a teenager.
>
> Her hair was always silky and blonde—mine was wiry and mousy. She had perfect vision—I wore thick prescription lenses with bifocals. She had a perfect hourglass figure—I was scrawny

with no butt and flat-chested. She had perfect teeth—I was still wearing braces. She could count the number of teenage pimples she had on one hand—I had to use acne soap and prescribed medication on a daily basis and still couldn't keep my breakouts under control. It's sad being on a first-name basis with your dermatologist. My sister was athletic and an honor student—I had no coordination and had to study three times harder than her just to maintain a B average.

    I hadn't seen my sister for a couple of years because she got a job overseas shortly after graduation. My parents and I went to the airport to pick her up, and I was extremely surprised by the drastic change in her appearance. She had gained quite a bit of weight and had dyed her hair a fake orangish-red color, which she had also cut super short. When she put on a pair of reading glasses to look at her cell phone, I was in a state of shock. But then I started thinking, *If she can change so drastically within a short period of time, then why couldn't I? Maybe I was like that ugly duckling who emerged as a beautiful white swan.*

The second door pictured is a beautifully painted brightly colored door with flowers flanking both sides. It is entitled "Behind the *After* Door" by Elise M.

    It was strange reversing rolls with my sister the following year. Now she was the one sitting on my bed watching me putting on makeup and getting ready for one of my dates. My teeth are now perfectly spaced, and my braces have been removed. My hormones and skin oils finally got under control, and I no longer have to deal with acne breakouts. My vision adjusted to where I could wear contacts, and my body finally had filled out in all the right places. Even my naturally blonde, but mousy, hair had become soft, radiant, and manageable.

My transformation didn't stop with my appearance however. The better I felt about myself, the better I treated others. The better I treated others, the more popular I became. Even my grades improved because of my change in attitude and more positive thinking. I was no longer dwelling on the negative in my life, which in turn made me more confident and productive. I even became more coordinated because my life was finally in balance.

I *had* turned into an even better version of my sister like I had hoped, but I will never forget the way I was before. Every day I pledge to be especially kind to all the other ugly ducklings waiting and wishing for their turn to emerge. It makes you feel so blessed.

It's good to hold onto your unattainable dreams because one day they may just magically come true—just like the beautiful white swan.

If you were just reading the *Before* and *After* door stories, you would believe that everything worked out well for Elise; however, Claire knows Elise's appearance and her sister's have not changed as it is written. At least she voiced her resentment toward her sister by reversing their roles in her stories, which is her way of opening up. The second story especially points to her dream of one day being attractive and accepted. Elise already understands the immense value of feeling good about yourself—even if it is only in her thoughts and dreams.

Chapter 6

Claire gets up and moves around for a bit before cleaning up the remains of her snack. After reading each of their stories so far, she paces back and forth as she tries to come up with a way to help each of her students work through their unique circumstances as a group, but their situations still seem to be too diverse to be bundled together under one plausible solution. She picks up her appetizer plate and loads it into the dishwasher before refilling her water bottle.

As much as Claire would love to reward her drained emotions with a nice long break, she feels too compelled to finish reading her students' stories that are currently in her possession.

The next picture is an oversized, bulky door with horizontal iron bars from top to bottom. It is entitled "Behind the *Prisoner in Her Own House* Door" by Todd S.

> Dottie was only thirteen when her older brother quit school his junior year and ran away. During the first six months he was gone, she was really angry at him for leaving her. It had always been just the two of them. They were the best of friends, and he promised he would always be there for her, but when he left, he didn't even have the decency to say goodbye or leave a note or anything. He just took off without so much as an inkling that he was leaving. She had no way to reach him and didn't have the foggiest idea where he had gone off to. He could be dead for all she

knew. "How could he abandon me like that? What happened? Why did my brother leave me?"

But her anger toward her brother was nothing compared to the animosity their parents had toward him. Every time the local police would stop by or call, her mother and father would always send her to her room while they discussed her brother, but she listened through the heating vents or with a glass held up to the door to decipher as many words as she could possibly make out from their muffled conversations.

From what she could gather, they had mentioned his college fund and some valuables, so he must have withdrawn most of the money from his college savings over the last six months and had taken several valuable items with him presumably to sell. Dottie noticed his duffel bag was no longer in his bedroom closet, so he must have had time to pack a bag, which meant it wasn't a spur-of-the-moment decision on his part. That in itself made her even more angry at him for not telling her he was considering leaving.

Her brother was last seen about two hundred miles from their home at a truck stop where he had hitched a ride with a truck driver. They were pretty sure it was him because he was wearing a red baseball cap, blue T-shirt, jean jacket, and a pair of jeans matching the description according to the authorities. Her brother was hoping to head east for some reason, but the truck driver was heading south so they had parted ways.

The longer her brother was gone, the stricter her parents became. It was as if one prisoner had escaped, so now the wardens were cracking down on all the other inmates.

Dottie was only allowed to attend school then come straight home after her last period—no more sporting events and after-school events, no get-togethers with her friends, and definitely no weekend activities. She could only use the Internet for school if one of her parents were with her making sure she was only working on her assigned homework. She had to stay in the house and was confined to her room every time her parents spoke to each other after dinner.

One of her classmates happened to be a sister to one of her brother's best friends, so she secretly passed a note through her classmate asking if he knew why her brother had left and where he planned on going.

Dottie was surprised to find out her brother suspected their father of losing or taking money somehow and was thinking about confronting him about it. His friend could not understand why he would have taken off though because he and several other friends had made special plans for that upcoming weekend that he was really excited about, plus he had just started dating a girl from their class that he had a huge crush on. Why would he intentionally sabotage his chances with her? His disappearance just didn't make sense to any of his friends.

Every chance Dottie got, she would collect information about their bank accounts and bills and even searched through his closet and dresser drawers to figure out which clothes he took with him. She thought she could contact the police anonymously with other clothing descriptions to help with their search; however, she didn't find any of his clothing missing, except for the pair of jeans, a blue T-shirt, his jean jacket, and red hat she had seen him in that day. In fact, she couldn't find anything of his missing so she couldn't figure out what he packed in his oversized duffel bag.

Every time her father stepped outside or her mother went to the bathroom, Dottie would snoop around the house some more trying to find clues as to why her brother had left. She finally remembered her brother's old hiding place in his bedroom closet under the carpeting, but she would have to wait until another time to check it out. A few days later, she got her opportunity.

The neighbors from across the street stopped over with a chicken casserole for their family. Her mother put it into the refrigerator but didn't want to invite them inside because the house wasn't picked up enough, so she brought a pitcher of iced tea, glasses, and cookies out to the front porch for the four of them to enjoy out there.

Dottie quickly raced into her brother's bedroom and pulled back the corner piece of carpet in his closet. There was a manila envelope stashed in his hiding place so she took it with her back to her bedroom to look at it. She made sure they were all still out on the front porch before she frantically opened the envelope. There were copies of the initial transfer to their college funds their grandparents had set up for each of them. The next page showed funds being withdrawn months before her brother had taken off, and in the margin was her brother's own handwriting adding up six substantial amounts all dated as well as a total dollar amount at the bottom of the page with *Dad???* underlined next to it. It was tens of thousands of dollars withdrawn from each of their college fund accounts but definitely not to be used toward tuition or books.

Not wanting to risk returning them to her brother's closet, Dottie put the pages back into the envelope, rolled it up, and securely fastened it with two thick rubber bands. She shoved her bulky mittens down the right sleeve of her quilted ski jacket with the elastic-gathered wrists and then slid the rolled-up envelope into the sleeve on top of them. Dottie felt they should be secure there until she can figure out what to do next.

The following week, Dottie contacted her brother's friend through his sister again. She said she found evidence pointing at possible wrongdoing by her father. She asked if he could take it to the police for her and just say her brother must have had someone leave it for him in his school locker because he recognizes it is in his handwriting. Dottie was relieved his friend agreed to help her out.

Dottie was so nervous leaving the house with the evidence the next morning and nearly fainted when her father gruffly called her back inside. She had forgotten to take her notebook with her for class so she quickly grabbed it off the breakfast table and ran out to catch the school bus. When she arrived at school, she was surprised to see her brother's friend parked in a temporary parking space near the bus drop off. He motioned for her to come to his car, and he took the envelope from her right then. He explained he wanted to leave his sister out of it just in case. Dottie mentioned to him that her brother's extra-large duffel bag is missing, but he hadn't taken any other clothing with him or anything else from the house for that matter.

From what she could gather during the following few days, her brother's friends spent several hours at the police station after school explaining why they didn't think their friend had run away. The police are currently investigating the cash withdrawals from the college accounts and looking into the father's activities over the last few years. Her mother is still under the impression their son took off with the money because there is no way her husband would do such an absurd, preposterous thing. Dottie is staying quiet for the time being. At this point, there is nothing left for her to do other than patiently wait.

Time will tell, but she knows deep down that her father was involved, and it is unlikely she will ever see her brother again. She prays her brother will forgive her for thinking he had left her intentionally, but most of all, she prays he didn't have to suffer.

Claire's emotions get the best of her after reading Todd's story. It's no wonder these teenagers are struggling. Claire is positive *Dottie* is actually Todd—somewhat clever she feels seeing Dot is close to Todd spelled backward. Each story deals with such intense subjects, but a father murdering his own son is unconscionable. No one could handle what they are going through by themselves. Claire just shakes her head as she reluctantly begins the next narration written by Ashley.

The picture is a Mediterranean-style door evoking another time and place. It is a welcoming chestnut door with curved stained wooden slats that resemble a smile. It is entitled "Behind the *First Chance We Get* Door" by Ashley R.

We used to laugh together, play together, travel together, and just *be* together when I was growing up. Mom, Dad, and I were so happy, and I had no doubt how much they loved me. I used to sneak out of my bedroom at night just so I could watch them washing and drying the dinner dishes together because they would always tenderly kiss each other after cleaning just about every plate or glass. I would dream of one day being as happily married as my parents.

Every morning, Dad would give us each a kiss on the cheek and tell us he loved us before leaving for work, and as soon as he got home, he would give Mom a kiss, but he'd always pick me up and swing me around in his arms to greet me.

Up until fifth grade, I would have my friends over to play after school or for a sleepover on weekends, and Mom and Dad would make everything feel so special for all of us. Whether it was hanging twinkly white lights up in the backyard for a preteen boy/girl birthday party or setting up make-your-own ice cream sundae stations, they always went out of their way to make everything perfect for us.

None of my friends will ever forget the haunted house they prepared for my Halloween sleepover in fourth grade. We screamed and laughed all night long, especially when Dad would hit the water pipes in the basement with a wooden spoon, warning us that something or someone was approaching. Usually it was just my mom knocking on the door with a fresh bowl of popcorn or homemade taffy apples, but even she would dress up like a vampire and try to bite our necks before leaving. I think my parents had just as much fun as we did that night.

The first time Dad didn't swing me around in his arms when he got home, I knew something was definitely wrong, but I wasn't sure what it was.

When I would secretly watch them affectionately wash and dry the dishes, it was only Mom at the sink then, while Dad sat at the kitchen table just lovingly watching her. Months went by, and I noticed he was having coughing fits all the time, but I was too afraid to ask what was happening. It didn't take long before I had my answer.

Dad was lying on the couch sleeping when I got home from school. There was a note from my mom on the kitchen table I was hesitant to read.

> Your dad is not feeling well. Let him sleep. I went to the pharmacy to pick something up for him. Be back soon.
>
> Love, Mom.

I was tiptoeing to my bedroom when Dad woke up coughing and called for me.

"Hey, Peanut," he said in a weakened voice and in between bouts of wheezing and coughing. "Can you come here for a minute?"

As I walked over to the couch, I knew he was going to give me an explanation, but I just wasn't prepared to hear it. I had been in complete denial since the first day he didn't spin me around because I didn't want to face the truth.

While stopping after several words to cough or catch his breath, he said, "Guess I can't keep this from you any longer, Peanut. I have cancer in my lungs, which is spreading, and even though the doctors are doing everything they can to help me, nothing has worked so far. I just want you to know how much I love you, and I will always be with you right here." My dad put his hand on my heart before I laid in his arms crying alongside him.

It was only a few weeks after that when he passed away. My mom and I tried to get on with our lives the best we could, but there was such a big hole left without him.

Mom wasn't good being on her own and needed someone to fill that void, and that's when Bob came into the picture. He was a likable guy around her age, and my mom seemed happy to have a husband again. At first, everything seemed fine having Bob in our lives, but within a few months, he showed his true colors to both of us.

It started one morning before school when I saw my mom removing a carton of eggs from the refrigerator, and I told her I didn't care for any eggs for breakfast—just cereal. Mom just smiled and started to put the carton back into the refrigerator until her husband abruptly spoke up.

"You'll eat what is served to you, young lady," he angrily blurted out. "You're having eggs whether you want them or not."

Mom looked afraid after hearing his angry voice and immediately brought the eggs back out to the counter. That evening, I sadly watched my mom doing the dinner dishes by herself, while Bob went into the living room to watch TV. When I went in the kitchen to help her, he yelled at me to get back to my room and finish my homework for school. My mom fearfully gestured for me to leave her and do what he said.

I watched my mother become a frightened slave to his demands, but I wasn't much better. Every day Bob would snap at me or full out yell at me just for the sake of arguing. Neither one of us could do anything right, but Mom and I kept trying so we might please him enough for him to stop his badgering.

I kept thinking to myself, *The first time he lays a hand on me or my mom will be his last.* But he was never physically abusive—only verbally. He would raise his opened hand or make a clenched fist as if he was going to slap or hit us, but he never actually followed through. It was his way of warning us to follow his instructions to the letter—or else. Still, nothing we could do was ever good enough for Bob.

The only bearable time was the hour and a half right after school when Bob was still at work, and my mom and I were alone together. My mom and I would always make the best of our special time while doing our chores or homework so he wouldn't have a reason to yell at us for that. We would talk about the way things used to be and fondly remember better times when Dad was still alive. We would turn on the radio and dance and sing but only during the first half hour just in case Bob decided to unexpectedly come home early.

Once I started high school, Bob would do spot checks of my room to make sure I didn't have any drugs hidden, or he would flip my textbooks and notebooks open and shake them to check for anything unrelated to school like illicit notes from boys. He would never allow me to wear what I wanted. He would always change something about my outfit even if it was just my pair of shoes or the belt I had chosen. Spot inspections became a daily routine.

My mom and I decided we needed something to look forward to in our lives, so one day after school, we planned our escape almost as if we were planning one of the elaborate parties we used to host. Right after high school graduation, Mom and I were going to leave our home and Bob behind. We couldn't write anything down, but we went over and over our plan so we wouldn't forget the smallest details.

All we needed to do was update our passports somehow, but Mom had already devised a possible solution for that. We were going to fly to Europe and live our lives abroad. I still had funds set aside for college, and Mom had my dad's life insurance money that Bob was not aware of. We were going to find a little house or apartment to rent, possibly in Italy or France, and she was going to get a job while I attended a culinary school there.

Mom suggested to Bob that we rent a fishing cabin in Canada for his birthday. She knew he liked to fish and missed having a boat. He thought it was a great idea, for once, and said he would look into it. We were both devastated when he brought home the brochure for the cabin he had rented in Minnesota just across the Pigeon River border from Ontario, Canada.

The following day, my mom was all smiles when I got home after school that day. Bob had agreed for her to take the car two counties away to go see my grandparents for their wedding anniversary, and he was allowing them to stay overnight since it was a Friday.

We were going to stop at the drugstore before heading to their house so we could get new passport pictures taken. My mom was so paranoid; she also mentioned, just in case he was following them, that they were going to buy an anniversary card and some balloons there as well.

If he did find out that they had updated their passports, Mom planned on telling him they only did it in case they drove over to the Canada side during his birthday fishing trip since it was so close.

Everything went according to our plan until our updated passports arrived at the house on a weekend. Bob retrieved the mail and was livid we had gone behind his back. Mom explained about possibly driving over to Canada during his fishing trip, but he didn't buy it for a second. He threw the envelope on the floor and took our updated passports with him into his bedroom. He returned with a Zippo lighter in his hand and started burning our new passports and then threw them over the fireplace grates. Mom and I watched as our dream of escape burned up in flames.

My stepdad is worse than ever now and has even threatened my mom with violence to keep her from divorcing him. I still plan on leaving as soon as graduation is over, but I'm definitely not going alone. I'm taking my mom with me no matter what.

Claire gets up from her chair and starts aimlessly meandering throughout her apartment. Ashley's story hits home for Claire. She knows all too well what it's like to have a controlling, manipulative, and verbally abusive stepfather and prays she will be able to help her resolve this caustic situation. She takes solace in the fact that her stepdad has never laid a hand on either one of them, yet, but she also knows that verbal abuse can cause just as much damage.

Chapter 7

When Claire walks by the unread stack of project papers, she starts to wonder why Chad would have chosen a pure white door with carved lilies on it. Even though she was once again planning on stopping for a while, her curiosity takes over, and Claire sits back down and starts reading.

Pictured is a pure white door with two large panels, each decorated with a center-carved lily. It is entitled "Behind the *Wanting to Wait* Door" by Chad T.

> My parents weren't very religious and never bothered taking me to church after I was baptized; however, every Sunday morning since I was five years old, my Grandma B would pick me up and take me to services with her. We always went out for breakfast after church so my parents were thrilled having a few hours to themselves each week.
>
> When I was old enough, she would drop me off at Sunday school after church, and then we would go out for an early lunch instead. I treasured my time with my Grandma B and would always be on my best behavior during the service to make her proud.
>
> Her health started rapidly deteriorating a couple of years ago, so she couldn't continue to take me to church anymore. I would always get a ride over to the nursing home at least once a

week with my mom so I could read Bible verses to her even though she was unresponsive most of the time due to her debilitating strokes. It was heartbreaking seeing her like that, and I prayed God would watch over her and take care of her. He honored my prayers less than a month later on my birthday. It was the greatest gift I ever received because I knew she was with him in heaven.

Even though I didn't physically attend church anymore, I still tried to be a Christian person and continued to read the Bible she gave me when I first started going with her to church. I knew I would never become one of the youth members who went door to door spreading the *Word*, but I kept my faith in my own way and kept it private from my parents because I knew they would never understand.

Since seventh grade, I had been with the same girlfriend. It started out at that age just holding hands when we were together or walking her home after school. Occasionally, we would kiss but not even to the point of making out. Eighth grade advanced our relationship. I would put my arm around her almost all the time we were with each other. Our kisses were a little longer but still controlled.

Freshman year was when the constant hugging began. We were always facing each other with our arms wrapped around each other, and our kisses were longer and more passionate. I was shocked the night she put my hand over her covered breast and held it there. I knew she wanted me to touch the other one, but I didn't feel right about it. Eventually, I caved into her wishes but stopped from doing anything further.

By spring, things radically changed. All my friends were egging me on to go further sexually with her because we had been together for such a long time. They felt it was only natural in the progression of our relationship. They were surprised we really hadn't done much of anything and made it sound like there was something wrong with me for not wanting to take advantage of the situation. Even my girlfriend kept questioning my love for her because I didn't want to have sex with her or even touch her under her clothing. Her friends were making her feel as though I didn't love her anymore if I didn't even want to touch her bare skin.

After the spring dance, a group of our friends went to a lake a couple hours away for the weekend. I decided to give in to some of her requests so I wouldn't lose her, but I refused to have intercourse with her even though she had a condom ready for me to use. When I told her again that I wanted to stay a virgin until I got married, she agreed through the weekend, but as soon as we got home, she broke up with me saying I must not love her and that she didn't want to wait that long. I know her friends' insinuations had a lot to do with her breakup decision because they compared sex to love: no sex, he doesn't love you; have sex, he does love you.

I was devastated and heartbroken after losing her. I loved her with all my heart and thought for sure we would get married and have a family someday. But I was just as devastated to find out she had sex with one of our mutual friends the same week we broke up—just to hurt me. I guess I didn't know her, or my friend, like I thought I did. Unfortunately, because the two of them were in our mutual group of friends, I was the one forced out. Not only did I lose my girlfriend, but I lost all of my other friends as well.

At this point, I'm steering clear of dating anyone. I don't understand why everyone pressures teenagers into having sex at such a young age. Why can't we live up to our faith and wait until after we are united in marriage in the eyes of God? What makes it so special if it becomes commonplace before being united in the church as husband and wife? No one ever considers the male being peer-pressured into having sex because it's usually the other way around.

Just because others are having sex because their friends are doesn't make it right. Am I so wrong wanting to wait?

Unfortunately, teens are being pressured into having sex long before they are mature enough to handle it. Chad is not wrong in wanting to wait, but Claire also understands what a tough battle he is going to be facing for years trying to hold onto his beliefs and wishes, especially when almost everyone else feels pressured into going against his strict standards. She hopes he'll be able to find someone who shares his wanting-to-wait views.

Claire continues reading even further when fully enticed by the bright-pink double door now facing her. She's definitely puzzled by his choice for his project door and is eager to find out why Aaron has chosen this particular door.

Pictured is a bright-pink double door with hand-painted decorative pulls on each side. It is entitled "Behind the *Nothing's Wrong with Me* Door" by Aaron C.

My entire childhood, I was your typical jock playing every type of sport imaginable, both district and traveling teams, and overlapping seasons on occasion. My dad and I would spend hours on the weekends practicing the current sport or running through the local park together. It didn't matter if it was soccer, baseball, basketball, or football; my parents always attended my games to cheer for me and the team.

Very early on, I knew I didn't have the same attraction toward girls that my friends all possessed. I just thought of the female sex as friends you hang out with but never as girlfriends. Even when I was at the proper age to ask someone to a school dance, I would only ask a girl to go with me because I knew once it came out that I preferred guys, my life would be forever changed.

I will never forget the first time I locked eyes with *him* freshman year. It was so surreal having an instant connection with someone who feels the same way. I had no doubt he was gay even though, like me, he did not have the stereotypical effeminate voice, arm movements, or gate exaggeratedly portrayed online or on TV. He was also a jock I had known and hung around with for years, but I had not been ready to open my eyes or admit my preference until then.

On the bus returning from a football game four towns away, we sat together toward the back of the bus. No one thought anything of it because we were just friends and teammates. We kept our voices down so no one would hear us but confirmed each other's assumptions then and there. We agreed to meet at his house after school on Monday—supposedly to work on science homework together. Both of his parents worked, and he didn't have any siblings, so we would be all alone to talk.

My parents had known him for years because of sports and really liked him. Of course they would have no objection to my going over to his house to study. My mom even packed us some healthy treats so we wouldn't get hungry before dinnertime.

That Monday, we got off the bus together at his stop about a mile from my house. Neither one of us said a word walking the two blocks to his two-story house. My heart was beating so fast with anticipation by the time he unlocked the front door and even faster once the door was shut behind him. We just looked into each other's eyes again and started affectionately kissing each other before we took another step. It was so much more comfortable than the few times I had tried kissing a girl.

He admitted he had a crush on me for a long time but had to wait until I was ready to accept him—and myself. He had also taken out several girls but knew they were not what he really wanted. We carried our backpacks up to his room and even took out our science books and the treats my mom had packed for us just in case someone came home early.

Our first time alone together, we took turns talking about the trials and stereotypes of being gay, and then we would go back to kissing. He said his mom suspected he might be but doesn't think his dad is aware. I told him my parents were oblivious to my sexual preferences and would not take the news very well. He also had never kissed a guy before but only because he was waiting for me.

I wondered if this was true love or just the rush of being with someone you're attracted to for the first time. All I wanted to do was kiss him, hold him, and never let go. I was so infatuated with him, it was going to be difficult keeping my feelings for him secretive at school and during sports together.

I couldn't even look his way in the school showers because I knew I would get turned on if I saw him showering naked. He knew what I was feeling and waited until I was at my locker before dropping his towel to the floor in front of his locker. It took everything I had to look away from him and keep my composure after seeing all of him, but I did return the favor by dropping my towel for him as well when it was safe to do so. We just looked at each other with a quick smile before getting dressed and heading out. It's funny how I've seen most of the other athletes naked from time to time, but they were like brothers to me. Unless there is that physical attraction between both of you, you don't even notice them because you could care less about their bodies.

Every few days we would meet each other secretly, sometimes just to exercise or practice our sports together but other times to kiss and hold each other. Neither one of us was ready to *come out of the closet* because if we had, high school would be miserable for both of us, and our families may not accept us.

Over the first year, we learned how to keep our emotions for each other in check until we were alone. We still didn't want to draw any attention to our relationship, so we wouldn't do anything repetitive together in public. But the closer we became, the harder it was to keep our secret from our parents, so we decided to come out to our parents—together. We truly loved each other and knew our relationship could not stay hidden forever—especially from our families.

The two of us actually drew straws to see which ones we told first, and I drew the short straw. I will never forget that Saturday morning. My dad was in the living room watching the sports channel, and Mom was in the kitchen putting away the breakfast dishes. They knew something was up when we asked them to stop what they were doing so we could have a talk.

There were tears at first, but I was surprised how calm they were about it. My dad explained that one of his best friends was gay and had confided in him. It helped him understand how we were feeling, and he knew there was nothing he could do to change our sexual preferences. He warned us of the ridicule and disapproval we would face once it got out, and that was his only objection to our being together. My mom was not as accepting, which greatly surprised me, but I think she was more worried about the consequences of our actions. By the time we left my house that morning, both of my parents gave each of us an accepting embrace, which felt like a huge, unexpected triumph.

When we left there to go talk to his parents, we took a detour to a secluded spot so we could kiss and hold each other in celebration of facing my parents and their cautious approval. We really didn't imagine we would have any issues with his parents, but we were totally wrong.

Neither one of his parents wanted their son to have a relationship with me or any other male. They kept saying we had been tempted by the devil and must redeem ourselves; it didn't mean anything because it was merely a test that we had failed because our faith was so weak; we should be ashamed and repentant for our thoughts and actions; and we should pray to wash away our lustful, evil sins.

It was against their religious beliefs to have a man love another man in that way, so there must be something wrong with us. They were so angered and greatly resented the fact we had brought shame to their household. They forbade him to see me or any other male from then on. His parents even came between us when he was going to walk me to the door.

That was the last time I saw him. His parents moved away, hoping that putting distance between us would change him back to a *normal* person. They made him attend church every day and see a therapist from their congregation, but it was futile. We would text each other every day, and I could sense how difficult it was for him to deal with his unaccepting, pious parents. We even discussed having him come to live with us, but when my parents discussed the idea with his parents, they furiously objected; realizing their son was still in contact with me, they proceeded to take his phone away from him as well.

The last words I had texted him were, "We'll figure something out. I love and miss you."

Weeks later, he managed to call and left me a voicemail: "I will always love you, and I am so sorry. My parents will never understand that there is nothing wrong with me."

His mother was the one to call our house to inform us he had taken his own life. She did not want us attending the funeral but gave us the location of his burial plot so I would be able to say goodbye because that was in her son's last written words along with his forgiveness of his parents.

It hasn't gotten any easier over time, but I still start out each day telling myself his final words to me: "There is nothing wrong with me." Maybe one day everyone will learn to accept those words as the truth. "There is nothing wrong with me."

Claire gets another tissue after finishing Aaron's inconsolable story. She knows how it feels to lose someone you love, and her heart goes out to him especially since he's so young and has already had to deal with such a profound loss—all because of a lack of acceptance for their sexual preferences.

She rereads Aaron's last sentence and shakes her head doubting if people's perceptions or religious beliefs will miraculously change toward acceptance but hopes he finds love again during his lifetime and forgiveness toward ignorance and obstinance.

With tears still running down her face, Claire picks up the next story and begins reading, but her cell phone ringing interrupts her. She smiles when she sees it's her oldest son calling. "Hello, Paul," she answers in her tearful voice.

"Mom, I'm really sorry I can't be with you tonight. I know this must be difficult for—" He immediately stops when he hears his mother chuckling.

"I'm crying over homework assignments, not our anniversary." Claire wipes her eyes and her nose before explaining further. "I can't deny that I feel lonely especially on our anniversary now, but not sad. Your dad and I had so many wonderful years together and lots of happy memories to fall back on."

"So why are you crying?" he inquires with great concern.

"Because it involves my sixteen special students, I can't really get into it, but let's just say the photos of doors you, Chase, and Anna took on our Mediterranean cruise have been a godsend. I'm using those pictures to help my troubled students open up, and some of their emotional and enlightening stories have brought me to tears."

"Sounds like they're finally confiding in you, Dr. Mom, but I'm sorry their stories are making you cry. Maybe you should take a break for a while so you don't become too overwhelmed. I'm sure you're on an emotional roller coaster today as it is."

"I'll be fine, Paul. Normally I can keep my sentiments in check while professionally working with patients, but reading my young students' firsthand accounts of their trials and tribulations have definitely brought me to my emotional limit. I just pray I'll be able to help them."

"I have no doubt in my mind, Mom. I still think you should take a little break and maybe reset your feelings before reading any more of them. I love you."

"Don't worry. I'll take your advice and stop for a bit. Thanks for calling, Paul. I love you too." Claire disconnects and gets out of her chair as her son suggested. Just as she's heading out of her bathroom to go into her kitchen, she looks at her ringing cell phone and chortles when she sees it's her youngest son and daughter-in-law calling her this time.

"Hi, Chase and Anna." She tries to hide her tittering, knowing her sons and daughter-in-law have been in communication about their *aging and alone* mother once again.

"Hi, Mom. What's up?"

Chapter 8

Claire is grateful to all of her students for turning in their "Behind the Door" narratives before their deadline. She tells her students to either work on other class assignments or talk quietly among themselves during the first period. She covertly watches as several of the students group together and socially converse back and forth with each other, while quite a few others work on other class assignments. She sees Toni resting her head on her desk, so she nonchalantly gets up to check on her.

"Trying to catch up on some sleep?" she asks when Toni opens her eyes.

Toni sluggishly responds, "I had a pretty rough night last night."

"I'm so sorry to hear that, Toni. Are you okay to stay, or would you prefer to go home?"

"I'd prefer to stay," Toni responds while closing her eyes again.

"That's fine. Try and get some sleep." Claire returns to her desk and looks back at Toni. She's been made aware that Toni has some major health issues, but that's all she's been privy to so far. Over the past couple of months, Toni has obviously been in a downward spiral with her health, and Claire is becoming greatly concerned about her, especially over the last few days. Toni seems to be having more difficulty with her speech, cognitive abilities, and motor skills. Her fatigue has compounded those issues, so Claire is relieved to see she is able to rest at least a little for now.

Claire doesn't even bother opening up her laptop to read another submission during school hours. She decides to wait until she is in the privacy of her own home. Her thoughts are interrupted when she hears some bursts of laughter within her classroom. She's surprised but happy to look up to see all but one of her students now huddled around in a circle enjoying each other's company while Toni continues resting off to one side of the classroom.

As soon as the bell rings, the fifteen disperse quickly, but Toni hasn't moved. Claire immediately heads over to her and whispers, "Toni, this period is over. Are you able to head to your next class?" There is no response from Toni, even after Claire shakes her on her shoulder a little. After checking Toni's pulse rate, Claire grabs her cell phone from her purse and calls the principal to see if he can shed some light on her condition or has special instructions regarding her ailing student.

The principal arrives within a minute with the school nurse. The nurse checks her vitals, while the principal contacts Toni's parents. When he ended his call, he approached the nurse and Claire to inform them Toni's parents were on their way to pick her up. "We're just to let her sleep until her parents arrive. Claire, if you want to head home, I can wait here for Toni's parents."

"No. I'd prefer to stay." Claire takes a seat next to Toni and holds her hand as they all wait together in silence.

When the Marchands arrive, they have a special transport chair with them for their daughter. As if professionally trained, the father gently lifts Toni out of the desk chair, while her mother holds her head as they transfer her to her mobile, custom-built chair. They raise her legs and lower her back and head before pushing her out to their mobility van parked right out front. The principal, the nurse, and Claire follow them out to their vehicle and wave to the appreciative parents as they drive away.

While heading back inside, the nurse heads down the first hall, but the principal walks back to the classroom with Claire and whispers, "Toni is dying, and we are to make her feel as comfortable and normal as possible for the remaining time she has with us. The parents didn't want anyone to know how serious her condition was because once people find out she's terminal, they treat her sympathetically. Toni does not want that from anyone."

Claire understands her wishes and is grateful for the confirmation of her assessment concerning her student. She grabs her purse, laptop, and tote bag and says goodbye to the principal before heading out. On her way home, Claire stops along the shoulder of a side street and sends a text message to her sons and her daughter-in-law: "Just wanted to tell you how much I love and appreciate the three of you." They all reply with their typical emojis before she continues driving home.

After Claire has changed her clothes and fixes a cup of coffee for herself, she sits down and begins reading Laura's story.

Pictured is a beautiful six-panel wooden door with windowpanes too high to see in or out of. It is entitled "Behind the *Our Little Secret* Door" by Laura J.

> Finding out your entire life has been one big lie has been almost unbearable. How could I have been such a naive fool for so many years?
>
> Up until my freshman year of high school, I did not have a social life. We lived on the outskirts of town, and my mother homeschooled me along with my two younger sisters, so I didn't have any other friends outside of my sisters to play with or talk to. Our school was so much fun though. We always dressed in costumes my mother had made depending on which subject we were studying: Juliet's high-collared dress and Tom Sawyer's rolled-up jeans with a white shirt and straw hat. For our history lessons, she always had all sorts of hats or accessories for us to wear: a top hat for Lincoln; a bicorne hat for Napoleon; a short mustache for Hitler; and Ben Franklin's eyeglasses and long-haired wig.
>
> We would pretend to travel to distant lands as we learned geography and geophysics or fly to outer space to study astronomy, astrophysics, and planetary science. We did all sorts of science projects in the basement or out in the backyard for the messiest or more sophisticated experiments.

Our mother made us eager to learn and participate in our classes every school day, but I was just as excited when my father returned home from work.

My life may have been sheltered from the outside world, but I was deliriously happy. My parents never let us watch TV because they didn't want us to be exposed to negative influences, but it didn't bother me because you can't miss too much of what you've never had. Since we were self-sustaining on our forty-acre homestead, we didn't require runs to the local stores for supplies or have contact with anyone other than each other, so I never questioned anything my parents told us. I had no reason to. I trusted them implicitly.

I was so shocked freshman year to find out that fathers don't show their love for their daughters by touching them sexually. Fathers touching daughters in that way was actually against the law and considered child abuse, but my father had always told me he touched me because he loved me so much and that is what all fathers did to show how much they love their little girls. But now I know why it was always *our little secret*. He had always explained that he just didn't want my sisters to know because they would have hurt feelings learning that I was his favorite little girl. I was his firstborn and the most beautiful in his eyes, so I was special. The only reason he didn't want me to bring it up to my mother was because she would be upset if he showed favoritism and didn't treat all of his girls equally. Now that I know he lied to me for my entire life, I'm not sure what to believe anymore.

He had been touching me for such a long time, and I enjoyed pleasing him. I'm not sure exactly when he started, but I would guess I was still a toddler. Even when he carried me upstairs to go to bed, he would hold me, so his hand was always inside my panties. He would always offer to help out with my bath time so my mother would be able to take care of my younger sisters, but now I know it was so he could have his hands all over me.

My father first showed himself to me when I was about four or five. He showed me how to please him several ways, and I was so excited to make him happy. The more I touched him, the more he showed me he loved me. The only time he looked disappointed with me was when I couldn't manage to roll the condom on him quick enough. He made me practice on him every day that week and wasn't gentle inside of me like he usually was.

Even after hearing what my father did to me was wrong, I was in denial. During our study period, I would go to the library and read about sexual abuse involving a parent and child. Everything I read confirmed that my father never told me the truth. He knew what he was doing was wrong, but he continued doing it anyway.

I ran copies of some of the sex abuse literature and confronted my mother after I got home from school. My father was still at work, and my sisters were harvesting some vegetables outside when I showed her several of the graphic and explicit articles. I could see the tears in her eyes when she told me she had started to suspect something because he always stayed inside with me while she and the girls were busy working outside but she didn't have any concrete evidence. She was too afraid and reluctant to confront him or me about it. When I explained to her in detail what he had done to me for years and what he had me do for him, she ran to the bathroom feeling nauseated. After throwing up countless times, she cleaned herself off, gave me a tight embrace, and told me everything would be all right. She then shakily picked up the phone to call the police.

I haven't seen my father since the police picked him up as soon as he arrived home that day. Even though I now know he lied to me my entire life, I hate myself for still desiring everything we did under *our little secret* because my father always made me feel so loved and appreciated. How will I ever be able to forgive my father—or myself? How will I ever be able to trust any man who tells me they love me? How will I ever be able to touch another man or be touched by another man without thinking of my father?

Even though Claire has tried to help patients cope with an entire spectrum of issues during her countless years as a therapist, the ones that have always bothered her the most are the ones involving abusive and deceitful parents. The questions Laura poses at the end of her story completely break down Claire emotionally. She is mentally spent and needs to recharge before reading any further. She closes up her laptop, changes into her running clothes, and grabs a bottle of water before heading out for a quick, necessary run.

When Claire reaches the park, she sees the sugar maple tree in the distance. It seems like a lifetime ago since she stood under that tree studying the sixteen remaining leaves, but it's only been less than a week. She takes her time returning home because she knows once she gets back, she'll be compelled to finish reading the rest of her students' traumatic and revealing stories.

Claire is so confused as to what to do now that her sixteen are opening up to her. First, she couldn't get them to divulge anything to her, and now that they have used their voices, she's not sure how she is going to be able to help them overcome their individual traumatic experiences. She looks up at the sky and sadly chuckles while saying, "Babe, we might need some divine intervention down here. Whatever you can do to help would be greatly appreciated. Love and miss you, Peter."

The wet fallen leaves have made the path she normally takes too slippery, so she slows down her pace to a fast walk and starts to head toward home. As she's unlocking her door, she turns around and looks at the colorful pastel doors across the street that gave her the initial *door* idea for the "Behind the Doors" project, but once inside, Claire becomes frustrated once again and groans out loud while attempting to figure out how she can help her sixteen students.

She takes out another bottle of refrigerated water and drinks half of it before removing her running clothes, showering, and getting redressed into her casual attire. She sits back down to read more of her students' startling revelations, but a text notification sounds from her phone she left in the other room. Claire gets back up to check it out before starting. She's apprehensive to read it when she sees it's from the principal:

> "Just got word Toni is alert and doing better. Doctor believes it was a reaction to her new meds."

She gratefully texts him back: "Glad she's doing better. Thank you for the update on Toni." Claire is relieved with the current news but also knows, all too well, the reality of what's to come. She finally opens her laptop to read the last few remaining submissions—starting with Victor's.

Behind the *Sixteen* Doors

Pictured are the local fire station's immense metal bay doors with windows three quarters of the way up. It is entitled "Behind the *Who Am I* Door" by Victor D.

My parents told me I was adopted as early as I could comprehend what that meant. I felt special because they said they chose me from all the other orphaned children. My mom and dad had tried to have children for years but couldn't conceive, so that's when I came into the picture. When I was five, they told me I was going to have a little brother. At first, I thought they were going to pick out another orphan, but then I watched my mom's belly grow bigger and bigger. Two years after my brother, my little sister came along.

We were a happy family, but you could tell just by my appearance that my coloring was quite a bit different than theirs. That's about the time my siblings questioned our parents about me. They told them I had been adopted before they were born. After that conversation, my siblings no longer wanted anything to do with me and resented the attention our parents gave me over them.

Every time I needed a new pair of shoes or a new baseball uniform or my bike repaired, my brother and sister would tell me I should just leave because I was costing their parents too much money. They gave me constant reminders that I was not one of them and I should go back to where I came from. My fighting and arguing with them became apparent to our parents who started siding with them even though they always lied to them about who had started the fights and what they were fighting about. It was two against one, so I always lost out to the two of them who sided together.

Freshman year I decided I was going to find out where I came from and hopefully find out why my parents gave me away. I asked my parents which adoption agency they went through, so I decided to start there.

My file consisted of two pages: the adoption record showing the day my parents adopted me and a small piece of paper clipped to the document. It was printed in Spanish: "Take care of Victor. His birthday is April 16th. I love him but can no longer take care of him." There was another notation on the back of the note with the words in English: "Dropped off at Station 53."

The clerk at the adoption agency explained that no questions were ever asked if a child was left at a fire or police station or a church. She grabbed her office phone book and advised me Station 53 was most likely the fire station located on the other side of town.

I used my allowance to call for a taxi because I didn't feel right asking my mom for a ride over there. It was disappointing after speaking with everyone there. Most of them were too young or hadn't worked there long enough. They felt bad for me and actually gave me a ride home on the fire truck. When I stepped off the rig, one of the guys jumped off right after me and sounded really excited when he thought of something that might help me. He told me to wait and wrote down the name of a lady who used to be the secretary there for the chief. She should have been working around that time and would be the one most likely to remember a baby being dropped off at the station. I barely slept that night because

I was so eager and excited to contact the former firehouse employee tomorrow.

The following day I tracked down the former secretary. She gave me a big hug when she found out who I was. Nothing else was left with me that day, but she did recall a nervous woman showing up the following week to make sure the baby had been found and was being taken care of—it was my birth mother.

The secretary explained further, "I made her come into the station with me, and we talked for quite a while. She was pregnant when she came here from Cuba. Her parents had disowned her for getting pregnant out of wedlock, so she made her way to our country with a mission group from the states. She had no money and couldn't get a job with a newborn baby, so she had no other choice except to give you away even though she desperately wanted to keep you. I told her the adoption agency we always worked with and told her you were well. After that, I never saw her again, but I remember her smiling knowing that you were going to be well cared for. That's what she wanted most of all. Oh, her name was Lena."

Even though I would probably never be able to find her, I was thrilled to find out her first name and that she was from Cuba. It was a part of the connection I was looking for. Plus, she was still pregnant when she arrived in the states with a mission group, so now I could check through hospital records in the area and find out which mission group was in Cuba back then.

It didn't take me long to find her with the correct date of birth and general location. The mission group was a different story. I went through almost twenty churches before finding the correct one. It was actually a mission group from our family's church, and two of the participants were my own loving parents. The plot thickens. When I asked the parishioner in charge of the mission if they remembered someone by the name of Lena, he looked puzzled by the question. "Did you ask your parents? They were the ones who sponsored her move to the states and—" He abruptly stops and then adds, "You'd better just talk to your parents."

When we sat down for dinner that night, I placed a sheet of paper across my plate with the name Lena written on it and nothing else. Both my mom and dad had a remorseful reaction seeing her name. Dinner that night was quiet, except for my siblings arguing with each other. As soon as they went back upstairs after dinner, my parents moved across from me at the table.

They explained again how they hadn't been able to conceive for years and when they met Lena, it was like an answer to their prayers. Lena and my birth father intended to marry, but he died in a fishing boat accident shortly after they got engaged. After meeting her in Cuba, they paid for her to return with them and promised Lena they would raise me as their own son, and she stayed with them until she went into labor. After I was born, they took care of her hospital expenses and gave her some cash to get by until she got a job if she would go along with their ruse. They had her drop me off at the fire station knowing I would then be given to the adoption agency run by one of their closest friends. The adoption papers went through right away, and outside of the mission participants and Lena, no one was the wiser.

I asked whatever happened to my birth mother, but they said they didn't know until a few years ago. They received a call from the hospital where I had been born. My parents were still listed as her emergency contact and were called when Lena was admitted after a terrible car accident involving a drunk driver and a carload of Cuban workers leaving the nursing home where they all worked one of the night shifts. She was unconscious and died shortly after they arrived at the hospital. They left a picture of me with her and told her all about me, hoping she could understand. They also took care of her burial because she had no one else—no one survived the accident.

My mom went into their bedroom and brought out a painted shoebox they had removed from Lena's apartment after she died. I was stunned to see stacks of pictures—all of me. She had been watching me for my entire life: all my first days of school, baseball games, playing in the yard or at the park, or swimming at the community pool. There were hundreds of photographs. When I opened the last envelope, I was overwhelmed looking at pictures of her with me in the nearby background. I had been so close to her so many times growing up, but I never knew.

My siblings quit picking on me as much when they were told about my birth father and Lena, my birth mother. Every week now, I go to the cemetery and talk to her. I don't know if I will ever forgive my parents for hiding the truth from me all these years, but I know I have forgiven Lena for giving me up for adoption. She was only thinking of what was best for me—her son, Victor.

"I'm glad Victor found his birth mother even though he only has photographs of her to hold onto now," Claire says to herself. "I hope in time he will forgive his parents and his siblings for their indiscretions as well."

She takes a few sips from her drink and opens up her laptop to begin reading Barry's story. Pictured is a dark-gray painted Dutch divided door with top and bottom halves that can operate independently. It is entitled "Behind the *Double-Faced* Door" by Barry F.

> Last year, I was the new kid at school—not because of a job transfer or a planned move but to shield me and my family from ridicule and harassment for a tragedy I was responsible for.
>
> Carrie had been my best friend since we were toddlers. Her mom babysat me when my mother was at work, so I was always with Carrie at her house. Once we started attending school, we always made sure we had the same teacher throughout grade school and middle school. We even signed up for the same school courses last year.
>
> Growing up, we were inseparable. Carrie and I had a special relationship and would support each other without question or thought. If I joined the baseball team, she was there cheering me on. If she wanted to do astronomy, we took turns using her telescope to look at the stars. Our parents never minded us spending so much time together because we acted more like siblings, so they didn't have to worry about us becoming sexually active with each other.
>
> Carrie and I were part of the popular group of kids throughout middle school and the summer before high school. The two of us were always included in any parties or get-togethers. Even though Carrie had a boyfriend and I had

a girlfriend, our partners tried not to be jealous of our close relationship because it was difficult separating ourselves within our mutual group of friends.

My parents were out of town on a business trip, and my older brother and his friends were over at our house for a pool party the week before school started. I hung around with them for a while, but I was only going to be a freshman, and they were all starting their senior year. One of his friends approached me and asked how I was going to spend my last free week of summer. I just shrugged my shoulders because our group hadn't really planned anything yet.

Later that night, he came into the kitchen where I was getting something to eat. He handed me a small cellophane bag with a couple small pills inside. "Here. Have some fun with your little friend before you go back to school."

The following night, Carrie and I contemplated trying the pills, but she kept saying we shouldn't. I was the one who talked her into taking it after a half hour of pleading. We went to our favorite secretive secluded area in the local park, and each of us took one of the pills. Nothing seemed to happen for a while, and we laughed about making such a big deal about it. Gradually, we both became extremely aware of our attraction to each other and started touching and kissing each other, but it was more like a dream state than reality. Someone else was controlling our thoughts and movements, but we got lost in each other. It was as though our bodies were melting into one another, and the sensations each of us were feeling were far beyond anything we had ever experienced.

Everything was heightened—our love for each other and all of our senses. I remember looking at her eyes as though I had never seen them before. I could focus on every eyelash and every one of her tiny freckles on the upper side of her sunburned cheeks. Carrie was mesmerized by my fingers and kept smiling as she studied them. Even the tall grasses surrounding us appeared to come alive as though each blade was dancing for our entertainment.

I wasn't able to get up yet, but Carrie wanted to dance for me. I watched her laughing as she spun around in her yellow sundress, waving her arms at her sides, until she fell back down on the soft ground next to me. She climbed on top of me and kissed me so hard, it nearly frightened me. When she got up again, she tried to help me up, but it was as if I was suctioned to the ground. The more I tried to get up, the heavier my body felt.

Carrie danced around again for a little bit, but I closed my eyes when she spun around and released the pulled blades of grass she was holding in her hand. By the time I opened them, Carrie was gone. I wanted to find her, but I still couldn't move. I could hear her singing and laughing, and I kept calling out to her, but she didn't come back. Carrie continued moving further and further away from where I was frozen in time, and I had no way to stop her.

After lying there for a while, my entire body suddenly felt like it was spinning out of control with centrifugal force. I thought my limbs were going to rip right off of my body in a million directions from the speed, but I didn't care. That's pretty much all I remember from that night with the exception of stumbling home after two o'clock in the morning, still hallucinating the entire way. Carrie's earlier presence seemed like a distant memory.

When I woke up late the next morning, I kept thinking back to the night before. Had we actually done all those sexual things to each other? Did she get home okay on her own? What happened to her after she left? Why the hell did I talk her into taking the drug?

It really scared me when I didn't hear back from Carrie after I texted her, which wasn't like her at all. After my second attempt, I started to panic and asked my brother to drive me over to the secluded area in the park to look for her. He was so pissed at me for taking the drug and even angrier at his friend for giving them to me in the first place. We looked all over the area but didn't find her. I didn't want to call her parents in case she hadn't made it home, so we combed the streets leading back to her house.

My brother asked for their number and finally called her house. He told Carrie's parents I had left the house this morning, and he was looking for me. He wanted to know if I was with Carrie. When he hung up his phone, he said Carrie wasn't feeling well and was still sleeping. I was so relieved she had made it home somehow last night on her own, but I was furious with myself for the whole stupid ordeal. I was smart enough to know better.

On our way home, my brother also made a call to his friend who gave us the pills. I was glad I wasn't on the other end of that scolding. He even terminated his friendship with him.

It was midafternoon before I heard back from Carrie. She was feeling better, so we decided to meet at the park halfway between our homes.

At first, it was awkward because we both semi-remembered what we had done to each other while under the influence of the pill, but our attraction for each other didn't wear off like the drugs. We ran toward the large monument in the park so we wouldn't be seen. It was all we could do to keep from having sex with each other. We stopped and looked at each other while breathing rapidly. The next thing I know, Carrie is offering drugs to me. She has an entire bag filled with similar pills from last night and a few unfamiliar others. She pops one in her mouth and swallows it before I can even respond.

I found out Carrie ended up with my brother's ex-friend after she left me. He was riding around with a few friends getting high and saw her dancing along the side of the road. He had given her another drug to try last night, and she bought the rest from him. I was mortified knowing she must have had sex with him to pay for the drugs because I knew for a fact she had no money on her to actually buy them.

My parents were still out of town, so I decided to bring her back to my house until the drug she just took wore off. I left her alone for a minute so I could go to the bathroom, but when I came back into the living room, she was gone. I heard my older brother shouting from his bedroom upstairs, so I ran up to his room and opened the door. Carrie was stark naked trying to climb all over him with her hand on his crotch. He was trying to push her away, but the drugs made her too strong for him. Between the two of us, we got her off of him and wrapped her up in his blanket until we could find her clothing. She was definitely hallucinating as she held her hand in front of her face and examined it inch by inch.

My brother started yelling at me for giving her a pill in the first place because now she's hooked and wants more. I knew he wasn't wrong. It was my fault I talked her into taking her first drug with me because I was too curious to flat out refuse it and too chicken to try it alone.

Over the next few months, I tried everything I could to get her to stop, but Carrie wouldn't listen to me anymore. She was using anything she could get a hold of just trying to keep that high going. I even spoke with her parents and confessed my initial part in it. They threw me out of the house immediately and told me never to step foot in there again and never to see or talk to Carrie again.

It was the day before Christmas break when I heard the sirens heading toward her house. My brother and I ran down there to see if it was Carrie, and I prayed she hadn't overdosed. My heart sank when I saw her on the gurney being taken away, but I was relieved to see she was still alive. Both of her parents saw me but didn't even have to say anything. Their angry, frightened facial expressions said it all.

Carrie is currently living at a ranch-style facility, where she goes to school and plays with other drug addicts. She now has the brain capacity of a ten-year-old due to her last overdose from a bad batch of pills.

The daily phone calls and constant badgering by her parents blaming me for their daughter's permanent disability finally forced us to move out of the area to avoid further ridicule from them and everyone else they managed to recruit to their side. They didn't just turn against me. They turned against my family too.

But they're right in one respect—it was my fault, and I will never forgive myself for what I did to my best friend. I truly love Carrie and miss her in my life. I never thought one mistake on my part would ruin the lives of everyone I loved. How can I expect them to forgive me? How can I ever forgive myself for something that unforgivable?

Claire is well aware how readily available drugs are in any school or through peers. She feels sad knowing how just one mistake can affect these teenagers for their entire life. Even just one pill tempting curiosity can cause so much destruction and heartbreak not only for the user but their family and loved ones too. She hopes one day Barry will learn to forgive himself for making one adolescent mistake and also hopes Carrie's family can find it in their hearts to forgive him too.

She also prays that the ex-friend supplier is punished for his part in dealing drugs to curious, impressionable youths. As far as Claire is concerned, drug dealers should be charged with attempted murder or murder for the irreversible, and sometimes lethal, damage inflicted on their naive, addicted victims.

When she looks at the next story, she sees the downward arrow on the door and can already tell by the graphics that this submission will be just as depressing. She decides to replenish her beverage and check her email before beginning Cory's story.

Pictured is a modern commercial red metal door with a black arrow pointing downward. It is entitled "Behind the *This Way to Your Future* Door" by Cory B.

I was happy once and thought for sure I would be happy again, but the older I get, the more difficult it becomes. It's not like I can pinpoint a specific time or a place when I realized I was becoming depressed. Maybe it was around puberty, but I suppose it really doesn't matter when you're contemplating suicide on a daily basis.

Once my mother started noticing the emotional swings, the highs and lows I was experiencing, she contacted our doctor who referred us to a psychological counseling facility specializing in depression.

That did not go over well with my father knowing that he is partially to blame for my ingrained low self-esteem. He was always bringing up my past failures or his utter disappointment in me for one reason or another. But mostly, I believe he despises me because I am not the son he expected me to be. I didn't turn out to be the athlete he had hoped to mentor to stardom like himself, and I wasn't the math wizard who could take over the financial legacy empire he was creating, and he resented me for that too. I am, in his words, "his biggest disappointment."

When you go from being a happy person to habitually being sad and have crying spells for no apparent reason, it's a warning sign you are definitely in trouble. But when you add those to all my other symptoms like frustration, anger, hopelessness, lack of interest, worthlessness, self-criticism and blame, sensitivity to rejection, lack of concentration, a future without hope, and recurring thoughts of death, it's understandable why my mother wanted to get me professional help.

At school, I went from getting straight *As* to incompletes. It didn't matter which class I was attending; I had a difficult time staying focused and occasionally would fall asleep before the end of the period. My appearance went from well-groomed and put together to unkept with offensive body odor. If I wasn't in the school nurse's office with some sort of aches and pains, I probably hadn't even bothered going to school at all.

The day I began prescribed medication treatment for depression was the day I disrupted class because I became irritated with the way the teacher was pacing back and forth in the classroom. I jumped out of my desk chair and started pacing right behind him without his knowledge until the other students in the classroom began laughing. He started yelling at me, and I yelled back even louder.

I'm hanging in here by a thread because my mother loved me enough to get me the help I needed in time, even though it cost my mother her marriage by doing so.

I no longer try to tattoo my own arms and legs, and I've completely stopped cutting myself, but I'm still working on all my other issues through my therapy sessions. I know I have to do this for myself, but I also want to prove to my mom that she was right to seek help for me. I'm not a lost cause as my father insists. I'm worth saving.

It's taken over a year, but I have managed to add one word to my vocabulary—hopeful.

So please don't judge me for being antisocial or for displaying frustration at times. It's just my awakening depression rearing its ugly head until I can get it back under control.

I pray none of you will ever have to deal with teen depression, but if I see any of the warning signs, I'll be sure to let you know.

Behind the *Sixteen* Doors

Claire is so proud of Cory for agreeing to accept help for his depression. She loves how he was so creative by personifying depression as if he has a split personality because that is exactly how it can *rear its ugly head*. Since Cory's narrative was fairly short in length, she decides to open Cassie's before taking a break.

Pictured are skinny, tall double doors in a pear shade of green. It is entitled "Behind the *Likely Pair* Door" By Cassie N.

> Ever since second grade, I was always the tallest student in the class and my shoe size was more like a man's. I would try to laugh off the stereotypical jokes making fun of my height, but after a while, I would just try to avoid people in general so I wouldn't have to subject myself to further ridicule.
>
> By the time I hit middle school, I was taller than all the boys in my class, and my feet had regrettably grown two more full sizes. It didn't matter if I was sitting or standing; I stuck out like a sore thumb towering over everyone, including my teachers.
>
> All I ever wanted was to have some normalcy, which didn't include being made fun of every minute of every day of my life. I went from being called the Jolly Green Giant to Gulliver to Goliath even though I should have been a giantess, a female giant, if they wanted to be gender accurate.
>
> Even my parents were extremely embarrassed to be seen out in public with me. They would always walk several paces in front of me and would go even faster if I started getting too close. We never went out to a restaurant for breakfast, lunch, or dinner because they knew I would be made fun of in public, but I knew the real reason—they just didn't want to be seen with

me. They never wanted to be associated with me because they were ashamed of the creature they had created.

It would almost make me laugh reading pamphlets and articles about self-esteem and body image issues. Every single one discussed being too fat or too skinny, too chesty or too flat, or acne or other cosmetic issues, but not once did they mention being too tall. If you're too fat, you can diet and exercise. If you're too skinny, you can eat better. If you get too chesty, you can have a breast reduction. If you're too flat, you can get implants. If you have acne or other cosmetic issues, there are medications to take for the problem or conceal it.

But what can you do when you are too tall and you have overgrown clown-sized feet? Absolutely nothing except pray you won't grow another inch taller and that your shoe size doesn't increase even further.

It wouldn't even be so bad if I was good at sports, but I'm too ashamed of myself to even try out when I imagine the spectators all laughing and pointing at me from the bleachers on both sides.

So for now, I get cleaned up and go to school without speaking with my parents. I attend school but always try to find a desk in the back of the room so my height isn't as obvious or obstructive, and I never socialize with anyone there.

After school, I go back home and spend the rest of the day and night confined to my nine-by-nine-foot bedroom. Every so often, my parents will eat dinner with me, especially for the holidays, but usually, they just yell upstairs for me

> to come down and get my dinner once they've finished with their own meals so they don't spoil their own appetites by having me present.
>
> How would you feel if even your own parents, the ones who brought you into this world, were too ashamed and embarrassed of you to be seen with you in public or so sickened by your appearance, they can't even spend time with you in the privacy of your own home?
>
> On a scale from 1 to 10—body image = 0, and self-esteem = 0—I don't even register.

"It's difficult enough dealing with self-esteem issues, but when you can't even find an ounce of support from your parents and they are a large part of your issues, it must be absolutely devastating. What a lonely existence for anyone, but especially a teenager," Claire says to herself. She is just about to stop reading to research gigantism and acromegaly to see if there are any treatment options or support groups to help Cassie, but her attention is diverted when she notices that Toni's final project piece is the only narration left to read.

Claire wonders why Toni was so adamant about having hers read last but hopes she'll find her answer once she has read through her submission.

> Dr. Claire, please allow me to go last in front of our class. After reading my story, I hope you will understand my request.
> Thank you.
>
> —Toni

Claire removes the sticky note from the stapled pages and begins to read. Pictured are massive cathedral-style, ornately carved wooden double doors with stained-glass heavenly depictions in a mullioned arch overhead. It is entitled "Behind the *Times Up* Door" by Toni M.

I had always wanted to travel to Europe, and my parents surprised me last year by taking me on a trip of a lifetime to Italy and France. In every museum and cathedral we visited, I began to feel even closer to God through the uplifting, spiritual religious paintings and the sacred scenes within the stained-glass artwork depicting a life with Christ.

For a long time, I was really angry with God. None of my prayers had been answered, but I didn't know why. I was a likable person. I attended church most Sundays, and my faith itself was unwavering. I never tried to hurt anyone verbally or physically. I was a good student and an even better daughter, so why wouldn't he listen to me?

I have prayed and prayed that my short existence on earth might matter—that it might mean something and that in some small way, I could make a difference. God answered me by giving me a voice, and I pray you listen to what I have to say.

Every day I get so infuriated watching other students my age just sliding by. Rarely do I ever see a student living up to his or her potential; however, the true slackers are not ashamed to run rampant throughout these hallways. I wonder what it would be like secretly listening to their parents discussing their nonperforming children. Are they as disappointed in them as I am, or do they not care anymore than their own apathetic offspring?

Watching my friends and family not living their life to the fullest is the most difficult of all. If I could, I would slap them each across the face and shout, "Wake up! Soak it all in every minute of each and every day. Grab as much as you can that life has to offer because once it's taken away from you, you'll know just how precious it truly is."

Between the tremors, the inability to concentrate, and the numbness in my arms, I can no longer live up to my potential. I was placed in this first-period experimental class with the rest of you because we all used to be at the top of our class, but now we are not for various reasons.

Out of all of you, I am the only one here with a good-enough excuse for my downfall. Sure, you've probably had traumatic experiences in your life that have utterly derailed you, but get back on track, and move forward as soon as you can. Don't waste another minute. Life is too valuable to squander even for a second.

I was diagnosed with glioblastoma multiforme a little over a year ago and was recently informed that I should live out the rest of my days or hours the best I can.

I don't want to be angry anymore, but listening to all of your petty comments and complaints every day makes it extremely difficult:

"I can't do anything with my hair today. It's so frustrating." Because of all the chemo and radiation treatments, I have worn a wig to cover my baldness since I became a teenager. I would love to have a head of hair so I can experience an *actual* bad hair day.

"I can't believe we have to read a whole chapter for history class before tomorrow." My mother has to read all my homework for me because my eyes won't focus on the printed words anymore. I would love to be able to read a whole chapter by myself and absorb what I'm reading.

"I can't believe I'm going to be stuck driving my brother's old hand-me-down car when I get my license." I have never even sat behind the wheel of a car. I will never be able to take driving lessons or even take a driving test. I would love to be able to drive *any* old vehicle down *any* street.

"My parents said I couldn't buy the dress I wanted for the dance because it was too expensive. They said I should get a job if I really want it." I would be thrilled wearing any dress because I will never know what it would be like to attend a school dance even though I have dreamt about going to one since I was a little girl. And how wonderful it would be to get a job after school and on weekends to earn a paycheck and be able to start paying back my parents for their unselfish generosity. If only I could pay them back for their tireless caregiving and the strain on their emotions my medical condition has caused them.

As a teenager, the worst complaint for me is when I hear you complain about your boyfriend or girlfriend. I would love to be in a relationship or experience a boyfriend's affectionate touch or kiss, but I never will—no holding hands, no college, no marriage, no children or grandchildren, no adult experiences whatsoever. My dreams for my future will never be realized—because my time is up.

Each of you needs to figure out what is truly valuable. Stop wasting your life with complaints and indecisions. Be achievers—not slackers. Be an upstander—not a spectator. Speak with kindness—not defamation. Work together—not alone. Be an example of good—not of wrongdoing. Together, I know you will find strength in your difficulties and learn to overcome your shortcomings. Never forget your past traumatic experiences, but don't let them define who you are. Use that pain and suffering to find your own voice. Begin each day by being grateful to be alive and grateful for what you have now. If you help each other, you'll learn to help yourself.

I chose this door because it reminds me of a painting I saw in Italy depicting the pearly gates of heaven. I do not know what exactly is behind my door, but it is the only thing I have left to believe in for myself when I die. Even if I'm no longer here with you physically, I will never stop believing in all of you. My short life *will* matter because you have heard my voice.

So when I'm gone, I hope you think of me often—because if you do, you might just try a little harder to live each day of your life to the fullest.

It is far too precious a gift to waste.

Claire sets her laptop with Toni's story down on the table and bursts out crying. Toni's words are her final wishes and will resonate more with her other fifteen students than anything she could ever say or do for them. They need to help themselves and help each other. That is the only way they are going to take their lives back and reach their fullest potential.

Chapter 9

The pastor was happily surprised to see Claire in attendance at church that Sunday morning. She hadn't returned since her husband had passed away years ago. As she's sitting toward the back of the church, she thinks about Erika staring over at her twin brother's coffin stationed next to the altar and imagines Chad as a perfectly behaved child sitting attentively in the pew next to his proud grandma.

She prays for each one of her students and their loved ones now that she has read all of their stories. She has a far better understanding of the intense personal issues each one has been struggling with. Claire says a special heartfelt prayer for Toni, now knowing her inevitable fate, and hopes everyone who hears Toni's voice will heed her strong message.

Tears begin rolling down Claire's face when she locks eyes with Erika who's leaving with her parents to go to the cemetery, but she's shocked when Erika slides in next to her on the pew and gives her an appreciative hug. Without a word, Erika smiles at her and then quickly catches up with her parents.

Claire remains inside the church praying for guidance on how to help her students now that she's heard their voices. She finally decides to leave before the pastor has a chance to corner her.

When Claire is about to drive away from the church grounds, she looks up and spots Erika leaving the cemetery with her parents. She is dumbfounded to see Erika's father's arm wrapped around her shoulder, and all three of them are smiling and talking civilly to each other while heading back to their car. She can't imagine what caused such a dramatic difference in such a short period of time but is very grateful to see the complete reversal—if Erika had spoken the truth about their relationship in her story.

On the way home, Claire decides to stop by the local grocery store to pick up a few items. As she's pulling out her grocery list, she hears a soft male voice behind her.

"Thank you, Dr. Claire," Brad gratefully says.

Claire turns to see her abandoned student, Brad, standing there in his grocery store uniform, smiling toward her. She notices his name tag says assistant manager under his name now, but she's not surprised at his promotion because he has such drive and determination at such a young age.

"And what may I ask are you thanking me for, Mr. Assistant Manager?" Claire inquires.

"Just thank you for listening and not judging," he responds with a smile. "May I help you find anything?"

"Thank you, Brad, but I think I know where everything is," she answers with a grateful smile.

From a distance, she watches Brad interacting with several shoppers and staff. She's so pleased to see him happy in his work and his communication with others, considering how much tragedy he has already had to face since his father died when he was only nine years old.

She finishes her shopping and puts her wallet back into her purse when Brad grabs her cart to help her out to her car. Their short conversation about the "Behind the Door" project is very enlightening to Claire, and she thanks Brad for sharing his experience with her. He gives her a quick, appreciative hug before returning to the store with her emptied cart.

On her way back home, Claire decides not to have anyone read their stories in class tomorrow. She now has something else in mind.

Chapter 10

As her first-period students file into the classroom after the first bell, Claire can sense a positive change in most of their appearances: no more slouching, no more buried faces, and no more apathetic expressions. They seem to be more energized and invigorated, and quite a few of them even smile or wave at her as they enter. They are all seated and appear to be quite attentive by the time the second bell rings.

Claire can hardly keep her emotions in check when she begins. "I've read all of your 'Behind the Door' stories." She takes her right hand and pats it over her heart while she tries to hold back her tears. "I know I had said that I was going to have you read yours to the class, but I have no right forcing you to do that. You are the only ones who can decide whether or not to share your stories with the class." She sees the students looking around the classroom as if curious what the others might decide.

"What I would like to do is find out how you felt before and after writing your 'Behind the Door' story. How did it feel to tell your story—to finally use your voice?" Claire inwardly gasps and almost collapses when she sees half of the class raise their hand in response. "Why don't we just start over here with you, Laura?" she suggests while taking a seat at the back of the room.

Laura gets up in front of the class holding a printout of her story. "The 'Behind the *Our Little Secret* Door' was my story. Before last week, I had never told anyone at school that my father had sexually abused me since I was a toddler. I had been homeschooled and had no other social contacts or interactions outside of our immediate family, so it was easy for my father to lie to me. He would always tell me that sexual touches and actions were the way all fathers show their love for their daughters."

Claire looks around the room and sees the other students' sympathetic reaction to Laura's story. They even clap for her when she says he's now in jail.

Laura continues, "When I first found out my father had actually been sexually abusing me my entire life, I was ashamed of my story, but once I read it for my mother and my sisters, I realized that maybe sharing my story would help others understand it wasn't their fault either. All we did was put our trust in a loved one with an illness. We shouldn't be punished for that." She leaves her copy of her story on the table near the front of the room in case anyone wants to read it.

Claire can see the other students agreeing with her as Laura takes her seat. Before she has a chance to say anything, Erika has already gotten up in front of the class with her own story. She shows everyone the picture of the old church doors and then tosses her story on top of Laura's.

"My parents always favored my twin brother, Ethan. He always knew exactly what to say or do to please them even though he rarely meant any of it. I was always blamed for everything because he could do nothing wrong in their eyes. But Ethan was a thrill chaser. The more difficult the stunt, the better he liked it. He became obsessed with his death-defying passion and was constantly pushing the boundaries."

Erika's voice starts to strain as she tries to hold back her tears. "My twin brother died while trying to do a swan dive off my bedroom balcony. My parents blamed me, and my father even insinuated I might have pushed him off because of my jealousy toward him. I never told them the truth about Ethan because I loved my twin brother and still wanted to protect him in my parents' eyes." Erika tries to smile at her classmates. "But all that changed last Friday. I had printed off my 'Behind the Door' story to read in front of class and had left it inside of my backpack. My mother came into my room to grab my gym clothes to wash and saw the photo of the door and the title 'Behind the *Doorway to Hell on Earth* Door.' She sat down on my bed and read my entire story. I was so startled when I entered my room and saw her holding it and crying. She asked me if it was all true, and all I could do was nod. All she could do was hug me and rock me back and forth, sobbing." Erika looks back at Dr. Claire and smiles.

"When my father got home from work, my mother showed it to him, and I could see the devastation on his face. I was so nervous entering the room when he called for me, but he reacted in the same manner. I was so happy to receive affection from my parents after such a long time but became distraught when they spoke to me about my twin brother, Ethan."

Erika breaks down when she tries to continue. Brad got up from his seat, gave her a tissue, and put his arm around her for support so she could continue. "I had been protecting Ethan my entire life, but I hated him when my parents spent hours telling me what Ethan had blamed me for in the past, and that was why he ended up becoming their favorite. He had told them lie after lie about me, but now they realized the lies were things he had done—not me. So if I hadn't written my story and my parents had never read it, my life wouldn't have changed for the better."

Brad and Erika give each other a big hug before sitting back down at their desks. Brad chuckles out loud when he realizes it's his turn and gets back up in front of everyone. He tosses his story on top of the others before starting, "I'd prefer if each of you would read my story, but I'll try to give you the main points. My dad was killed in the service when I was nine. My mom couldn't deal with the loss and became an alcoholic, which forced me to take over our household responsibilities by the time I was twelve. I haven't seen my mother for a long time, but I didn't report the fact that she abandoned me because I didn't want to go into foster care."

He takes a deep breath before continuing, "My story is similar to Erika's. I was at work Friday night and was alone on my dinner break in the back room. My boss came in and sat down with me. When he asked what I was reading, I decided to show it to him. I really liked and trusted my boss, and I thought maybe he could offer some advice. I knew he could report me for living on my own, but

I felt compelled to share my story." Brad looks back at Claire and smiles from ear to ear.

"Even though I never wanted to move out of my home, I have since changed my mind. It's about time I had a little normalcy in my life. I found out that night that my boss and his wife were currently fostering two children and were looking into adding another. When he wrapped his arm around me and asked me to be a part of his family, I can't remember the last time I was that happy and felt so loved. And he's thrilled because the other foster children they have are girls. Since I'm what they would consider a *special circumstance*, they have already been approved to take me in. I'll be having a sale at my former house next weekend if anyone wants to help out." Brad takes his seat, and Claire hears Erika, Victor, and several others offer to help him.

Claire gets up from the back before they continue. "It's getting close to the end of the first period, so we should probably stop right here." She's shocked to hear objections verbalized from the entire class. Several students say they would rather finish all the stories than go to their other classes, and everyone agrees. Claire is overwhelmed by their enthusiasm and asks each one individually what they have going on the rest of the day.

It's five minutes before the bell is going to ring for the next period, and she tells all of her students to stay put until she returns. Claire runs down to the principal's office and rushes inside. "We're having a major breakthrough with my first period class, and we would like to continue our class throughout the rest of the day." He looks dumbfounded at her request, but when she motions for him to make a decision quickly, he agrees and tells her he'll make an announcement so the other teachers are aware of her students' excused absence.

Claire races back down the hallways and reaches her room just as the first bell rings to dismiss the first period. Her students cheer when they hear the principal make his announcement: "All students in Dr. Claire's first-period class shall remain in that classroom for the remainder of the day. All other teachers are to excuse those students from their other classes today."

She returns to her chair at the back of the room as the next students take their turn discussing everything from bullying and experimenting with drugs to the warning signs of depression or saving themselves for marriage—and all before breaking for lunch. It's almost surreal looking at her students laughing together, sharing their food, and sympathizing with one another.

Claire notices Toni is struggling to control her body tremors and facial muscles, but the class doesn't notice them yet. She quickly gets out of her chair and sits between Toni and the other students. Claire takes her by the hands and asks, "What would you like to do, Toni?"

Toni's speech is slurred and staggered when she answers, "I would like to stay, but I think God might have other plans. Will you read mine now so I can feel a part of the group?" Claire tearfully agrees but tells Toni she's calling her parents first. Toni smiles in agreement.

After Claire makes her call, she asks everyone to take their seats and listen carefully. With tears running down her cheeks, she informs them that Toni has asked her to read her story to the class for her. Toni continues to smile at her for encouragement as Claire emotionally reads her "Behind the *Times Up* Door" story. As she continues, each of the students takes turns going over to Toni to give her a hug or a kiss or both, but Toni continues to smile. When Claire finishes it, she places it on the pile with the others and goes back to stay with Toni until her parents arrive.

They hear the ambulance sirens approaching, and Toni weakly says, "My ride is here." Toni looks directly into Claire's eyes and says, "Thank you for being my voice." Her parents rush into the classroom and tell her how much they love her before Toni closes her eyes for the very last time.

All the remaining fifteen students are standing by each other, some holding each other's hands or tearfully hugging as the paramedics rush Toni out of the classroom. With the exception of some sniffling, there's an eerie calm that settles over the room. Claire isn't quite sure what to do under the circumstances because she doesn't want to push her students too far today, but she also doesn't want to lose this momentum.

By the time she turns around toward her students, she stops when Emily suddenly breaks the silence. "I think we should honor what Toni has requested. We shouldn't waste another minute because life IS too precious."

All the students immediately return to their desks, and Claire sits down in Toni's desk chair as Emily immediately begins, "I was raped multiple times by an upperclassman on my fourteenth birthday. I kept it to myself until I found out I was pregnant. Yes, you can get pregnant the same time you lose your virginity. He and his father weren't going to help me, but his mother did. She's the one who took me to get an abortion and paid for all of my expenses. My parents still don't know I was raped, got pregnant, and chose to have an abortion, but his mother and I have formed a special bond together. We can't always deal with things by ourselves. Sometimes, we need a shoulder to cry on or someone to just listen. I know I'm not the only one who has been raped or is dealing with teen pregnancy in this school."

Emily picks up the pile of stories and places hers on top. She waves them all in front of her while saying, "We need to share our stories. I wish everyone could read our stories. We need others to know they are not alone." She gently places the stories back on the table and turns to head back to her desk chair.

Claire notices all the genuine support she receives from the other students as she makes her way back to her desk. She can tell the majority of the students agree with her.

Todd gets up and stands in front of the class. "I'm not sure how my story could help someone other than myself, and under the circumstances, it cannot be truthfully told yet. My story tells of a girl named Dottie who is very close to her older brother, but one day, her brother leaves without saying goodbye, and she's heartbroken. But over time, she finds out while snooping on her parents' conversations and speaking with her brother's best friend that he may not have run away after all."

Todd takes a deep breath before continuing, "Dottie found out her father had been withdrawing tens of thousands of dollars from each of their college funds and had possibly stolen some of their heirloom valuables as well. Dottie's mother believed what her husband had told her and never suspected her husband of doing anything wrong. She was under the assumption that her son had taken the money along with the valuables and ran away." Todd begins to tear up.

"With the evidence Dottie had accumulated and with the help of her brother's friends, the police are now looking into her father as the prime suspect in the disappearance of her brother, the valuables, and the college funds, but Dottie already knows her brother is dead and her father is the one who killed him."

Tears start streaming down his face as he tosses his story onto the pile. "When I wrote it, I used the name Dottie instead of putting my own name down. I wasn't ready to accept that my father had killed my brother, and I would probably never know the entire truth. But after a day like today with all of you and Toni, I'm ready for anything life throws at me. Bring it on."

Todd's classmates cheer for him as he returns to his desk. The remaining students get up to give a synopsis of their stories covering other teenager issues they have been dealing with and then add their own stories to the pile.

Once they are finished, Claire finally gets up to face her class again. "I am so proud of each and every one of you. I know how much courage that took just to write your stories and even more strength to share them with me and your classmates. Did the 'Behind the Door' stories help you?" She looks around the room and sees all of them nodding affirmatively. "By sharing your stories with the class, did it help you?" She gets the same response, but it doesn't stop there.

One after another, her students begin to throw out suggestions. "We should make our stories readily available to other students."

"I think we should print up our stories in a book for the library and counselor's office."

"Maybe we could organize an assembly covering issues teenagers continue to face over and over. I know we aren't the only ones going through this. I believe our stories would be beneficial to the entire student body."

Claire tries to settle her students down a bit even though their newfound enthusiasm is truly inspiring. "You all have wonderful ideas, but have you considered the consequences? For some of you, are you ready for your parents to find out your story? What about your family? Will your peers look at you differently or be less accepting? What about your other teachers?"

Brad stands up and waits for Claire to acknowledge him. He looks at the other students. "We each have to make our own decision, but my life changed by sharing my story with just one other person. Imagine the domino effect we could have on others just by putting ourselves out there. And if there are repercussions, we've always got each other, and I'm sure Toni's going to help us along the way. I would like to share my story in front of all the other students at an assembly."

Erika joins him standing. "If my parents disown me because I was raped, then they never truly loved me. I'm in."

"I know my mother and sisters would back me in a heartbeat," Laura says. "Sexual abuse by a parent or family member needs to be stopped."

Dave stands up and adds, "Everyone needs to know the effect bullying can have on a person—no matter what their age."

One by one, they stand to voice their opinion. Todd rises last. "Since I can't share mine until the police investigation is over, may I read Toni's? I think everyone should hear it."

Claire finally has them all return to their seats. "I'm not going to say a word about this to anyone until you have a chance to really think it over. What may feel like a great decision today might not tomorrow. Give yourselves some time to consider what you are planning to do, and we will discuss it over the next few days."

She looks over at Emily and adds, "I don't think your parents should find out the truth during or after the assembly, if there is one. If you would like, I will be glad to face them with you. And that goes for the rest of you too. I'm here for you, however I may help you. Based on some of your stories, it might be just as difficult, or more so, facing your parents as it was to write your own story. Please take your printed submissions home with you in case you wish to discuss them with your families, and feel free to call me anytime if you need some additional support. I'll also be stopping by to see Toni's parents tonight and will let you know when I hear of any arrangements or special wishes. I am so very, very proud of all of you."

The bell rings announcing the end of the last period. All her students chuckle as they try to do a group hug before departing and even invite Dr. Claire to be a part of it. Claire watches as they file out the door with compassionate smiles on their faces for the very first time. Once she shuts the classroom door, Claire collapses on the floor, sobbing from such an emotional, unexpected, breakthrough day but also because it is such a sad day due to Toni's passing.

She quickly wipes her eyes when she hears a knock on the door. The principal slowly opens it and enters but is startled when he sees her on the floor next to the door. He quickly closes the door and kneels down beside her. "Are you okay, Claire?" All she can do is nod. He helps her up off the floor and gives her a sympathetic embrace, which makes her cry even more. "I'm so sorry about Toni. Are your students handling it okay?"

She softly chuckles after hearing his question. "They're handling everything much better than I expected," Claire responds. They both sit down and talk for a few minutes.

"I know I'm not privy to what goes on in your classroom but wanted to know how it went with your special door project and your extra time today with your students."

"It ended up being a miraculous day—even for Toni." She is purposely vague with her response. "I'm very proud of my sixteen students." Claire smiles thinking over today's discussions. "So very proud."

"Well, I'm glad it went well, and again, I'm so sorry about Toni," he says as he exits the classroom.

Claire picks up her cell phone and calls Toni's parents. "Would it be all right if I stopped by sometime? I'd like to talk to you about the paper Toni had written for class." She waits for a response and then informs them, "I'll be right over."

Toni's story is the only one remaining on the table. Claire picks it up and holds it tightly against her chest for a minute, before she puts it into her tote bag and exits her classroom.

Chapter 11

"Good morning," Claire greets all of her enthusiastic students as they begin filing into their first-period classroom. It only took her students one night and a day to discuss their "Behind the Door" stories with their families and for all of them to receive their parents' reluctant permission allowing their children to share their personal traumatic experiences with the entire student body and other special invitees.

Over the next few weeks, Claire and her remaining fifteen students prepare for their upcoming school assembly. In order to best present their stories, the students work together revising each of their original works so their words transform into the most impactful and relevant message for everyone in attendance. None of their collaborated revisions change the essence of their original story. They only modify the wording in order to emphasize and highlight their messages. Toni's story is the only one they unanimously chose to keep exactly as written.

They even recruit some of the audio/visual (A/V) students to record Toni's examples of petty comments made by students—"I can't do anything with my hair today"—and play them from different speaker locations throughout the auditorium's tiered seating while timing them perfectly during Todd's reading of Toni's story. During their trial run, they were all thrilled to hear how the recorded voices seem to reverberate and appear as if anyone in the audience could have made the remarks.

Each of the parents or guardians of the *sixteen* were given several options to watch the preview of the assembly. They could either attend the dress rehearsal the week before or view a taped version of an individual speaker in the privacy of their own home, or they could read all the students' revised stories to be aired or any combination of those options. After their initial shock as to the transparency of the content being read and full exposure involving their own teenagers, most of the parents decided they would also be attending the assembly to show their love and support for their courageous student.

The profound effect these traumatic stories had on their families was astonishing. Unfortunately, not every parent was pleased with the way they were personally being portrayed and felt they were being unfairly targeted and misjudged. Those individuals chose to refrain from the public humiliation they would potentially incur once their child's story was voiced at the assembly. It didn't come as much of a surprise because those parents were also the ones who refused to accept any responsibility for their inexcusable actions and probably never will. At least they didn't stop their child from telling their story at the assembly.

Claire was also thrilled with the A/V department students for their creative assistance displaying the photographed doors and project titles on the overhead screens as well as all the spotlights and low lights they had rigged up prior to the dress rehearsal and assembly presentation. Even her old classmate, Brad, had managed to find student volunteers to set up the reserved seating areas for the assembly along with sixteen chairs facing the podium for her and her remaining fifteen students.

Within several weeks, the parental previews are completed; the stories have been revised and approved by all of the classmates working together as a team; all the special invitations have been received and accepted, and her entire class was honored to attend Toni's funeral together.

That evening, Claire took a walk to clear her mind and couldn't help but chortle when she saw the leafless sugar maple tree in the park. She wonders if it was fate that made her notice the sixteen remaining leaves on that tree not that long ago, or was it coincidence or possibly even divine intervention considering the miraculous results that have already ensued? She looks down at the indiscernible layered leaves lying on the ground but smiles because she knows her *sixteen* will never fall through the cracks or become lost in the system now that they have opened up and shared what they had been hiding.

Chapter 12

Claire takes one more look around the auditorium to make sure everything is properly set up for their upcoming event. She completes a last-minute sound and lighting check with the A/V department students assigned to assist with their school assembly. She chuckles on the inside when she sees the boxes of tissues her students have considerately placed at the end of each row in the tiered audience knowing how many tissues she had gone through while reading their stories for the very first time.

Both front-end sections are marked reserved for family members, special invitees, school board members, and district and state representatives per her students' request. On the main floor, she sees the chairs that have been lined up facing the podium for Claire's students along with one for herself and double-checks to make sure their revised printed stories are lying on their respective chairs. The student videographer is already standing by, the podium is centered on the main floor with a spotlight aimed at it, and two pulldown screens are locked into position above and behind it showing the prominent assembly title, "Behind Our Doors," in large-enough letters to cover from one side of the double screen to the other.

When the first bell rings to call the assembly, Claire anxiously scurries across the floor to join her students. She's overwhelmed when she sees her two sons and daughter-in-law arriving to support her, and they all greet her with a hug and a kiss. They quickly wish her well and then take their place toward the back of the reserved section along with the family members who had been visiting with their children backstage. Even though Claire's aware that several parents are intentionally absent today, she's so glad all the parents were given a preview and know what to expect. That is more than her own family members and anyone else attending this special assembly, and she prays it will be well received.

Claire looks over and sees Toni's parents being seated in the front row of the reserved section. They affectionately smile and wave over to her and her students. On the opposite side of the auditorium, she sees the principal escorting the school board members and school staff to their reserved section. Claire gestures for her students to take their assigned seats as she advances to the podium once the second bell rings out across the auditorium.

As soon as everyone has been seated, the lights go dim and then brighten several times before everything goes black throughout the auditorium except for the two pulled-down screens showing the words "Behind Our Doors."

The spotlight illuminates and shines down on Claire at the podium while the lettering behind her is artfully swirled and scattered in every possible direction until it is off the screen. The individual door photos begin to race across the screen and start to overlap in almost a frenzy before settling down on the overhead screens showing all of the eighteen doors chosen by the sixteen students.

"Good afternoon. For those of you who do not know me, my name is Dr. Claire Thompson. Last summer, I was presented with an unprecedented challenge for the current academic year. The school board seemed to think that with my suicide and trauma group therapy background, I would be a good candidate to try to figure out why these sixteen students seated in front of me had changed from exceptionally good students to failing, apathetic slackers. Even though there are physically only fifteen of these teenagers present here today, Toni Marchand's spirit lives on through these students, and her powerful voice will also be heard here today."

Claire turns to look up at the screens and stands silent as the back screens post Toni's picture and date of birth and death. It slowly weaves in and out of all the photos and disappears behind the pictured doors.

Claire turns back around to the microphone. "It took me almost two months to get my students to open up, but now I can't silence them, and I definitely wouldn't want to, so please be respectful and let their voices be heard." She claps, and so does the audience, as she takes her seat while Brad is first to speak at the podium.

"Several weeks ago, all of us entered our first-period class and were intrigued by unique photographs of doors hanging up all around the room, but none of us wanted to admit to our curiosity. Dr. Claire told us to examine the pictures of the doors and choose one that would best represent our story. Did they remind us of anything—a time or a place—our past or possibly our future? What happens behind our door? What story do we wish to tell? What do we need to say with our voice? What's hiding behind our door? She kept repeating the words over and over until we had all made our choices. So these are the 'Behind the Door' stories we needed to tell."

Brad sits down, and Emily takes the podium as all the doors seem to dissolve away, except for her two choices. On the back screen is displayed both doors she had chosen with the titles of both doors shown above them.

As her first door and title move forward, Emily bravely begins telling her story, "I will never forget my fourteenth birthday…"

Claire watches as each of her students get up to read their story once their door and title take the forefront on the overhead screens. She has her back to everyone else in attendance and wouldn't be able to see their reactions anyway because of the darkness enveloping the stadium-type seating. But she can hear the muffled crying and sniffling behind her and from both of the reserved sections. As her students continue to discuss anything from rape, teen pregnancy, abandonment, depression, low self-esteem, bullying, cyber relationships, religious beliefs, parental sexual abuse, death of loved ones, parental or sibling deceit, illegal drugs, sexual preferences, and social acceptance, Claire hears all the gasping, sighing, disgusted, and distraught sounds emanating from the audience as they listen intently to each of her students' intense and graphic personal stories. She is beyond grateful for the respect everyone has shown her students. Normally, there are the usual degrading outbursts by a select few attention getters during assemblies, but today, they have thankfully remained silent.

She wonders how many of the other students can relate to some of these narratives or are contemplating sharing their own stories and hopes they come forward for help. Claire also speculates as to how many students will think twice about bullying someone or mocking their peers after hearing what might happen firsthand if they push someone too far.

The portrait of Toni along with her chosen door appears on the back screens. Todd walks up to the podium. "I cannot read my own story due to special circumstances but have asked to read Toni's story for her." Todd looks over at Toni's parents and smiles.

The remaining students and Claire stand and gather on either side of him as the lights begin to gradually illuminate across the audience.

Emily breaks down for a minute when she sees her rapist's mother holding hands with her own mother in the family section. Both mothers are proudly smiling over at her. Claire wraps her arm around Emily for support as Todd begins. All fifteen of them manage to keep it together as he passionately reads her powerful words. When he reaches the *petty complaints*, the recorded voices are played in perfect timing prior to Toni's responding comments read by Todd. When he finishes, her door and photo are blended in with all the reappearing others.

Brad retakes the podium. "Sharing your story with one person can change your life for the better. We wanted to share our stories because so many teenagers are facing horrific, unimaginable issues every day—alone and afraid. We hope our presentation has taught all of the students assembled here that you do have a voice. You are not alone. We will not judge you. We are all here to help. Thank you all for listening to our stories. Now it's time for you to use *your* voice to tell *your* own story. What's behind *your* door?"

All the photographs of the doors shrink down and come together to form one large door with the same question displayed: "What's behind *your* door?"

Claire and her students give each other a group hug while the audience gives them a tearful standing ovation as the auditorium lights reach their full capacity. They can see all the emotional students, family, staff, and board members wiping their eyes and blowing their noses in between clapping and resounding cheers.

Their family and friends immediately join them on the floor to congratulate all of them on their successful program. Off to the side, Claire is speaking with Paul, Chase, and Anna when she starts to see hundreds of students joining them on the floor. Most of the students head directly over to a specific student whom they can relate to and start asking questions or telling them about their own troubling situation. Her family sees how busy she's about to become and decide to leave her for the time being as the school board members approach and congratulate her on such an informative and enlightening program.

Claire nods toward her students. "It was their idea to speak out. I just got them talking."

Chapter 13

After their extremely successful assembly, Claire lost her job teaching her first-period students. Now she lets her students do the teaching, and she just supervises. They have opened up their classroom to anyone who wishes to tell their story without judgment or ridicule or to just stop by for some friendly teenage advice or comradery.

Within a few months of their assembly, new friendships were forged for some, and justice was lawfully served for others.

Todd's father finally confessed to accidentally killing his son and was charged with involuntary manslaughter and felony grand theft. His brother's body was found buried in the field next to their house, along with his oversized duffel bag still housing a few of the heirloom valuables and a portion of the cash the father had stolen from their college funds. Todd's brother had never left him. He had never even left the neighborhood. The driver who had reported seeing Todd's brother two hundred miles away actually saw Todd's father wearing his son's clothing and red hat to get the attention off himself and onto his son instead. Dr. Claire and all of Todd's classmates attended his brother's funeral together to show their support. Even Toni Marchand's parents were there to express their sincere condolences to Todd—their daughter's voice.

Aaron was totally shocked when his teammates and coaches all showed up at his house after the game the following weekend. As their way of showing Aaron unwavering support and sympathy for his tragic loss, they drove him to his boyfriend's gravesite to personally pay their respects alongside him. Several cars with parents and other students, including his first-period classmates and Dr. Claire, followed the school bus as they made their way two counties over to mourn their former fallen teammate together. With the support of his friends and teammates, it was the first time Aaron truly believed the statement "There is nothing wrong with me."

Emily's rapist was so overwrought and ashamed seeing his own mother holding hands with Emily's mother at the assembly, he turned himself into the police right after. None of his victims came forth to press charges, including Emily, because he was punishing himself far more than any correctional institute for sex offenders ever could. He did request his name be added to the sexual offender database even though no charges have been made against him, and he is now volunteering his time doing community service on his own to try to make up for all the wrongs he ever did to others. He has already apologized to all of his victims and is continuing to go to therapy and staying on his prescription regimen. Even his father has come to terms with his son's heinous sexual conquests and has joined his son's charitable volunteer work.

Instead of his normal pretense showing an opened flat hand or the gesture of a clenched fist as a warning, Ashley's stepfather, Bob, stepped over the line and physically struck her and her mother repeatedly after reading Ashley's deliberate assault on his character. That was the breaking point for all of them. Her bruised and battered mother finally mustered up enough courage to tell him to leave or she would call the police and have him arrested on assault charges. She also filed for divorce and is holding onto photos of their injuries in case he contests it. Ashley and her mom are thrilled to have him out of the house. The two of them are already happily planning their move to Europe in two years right after Ashley's graduation and have already requested new passports to replace the ones Bob burned up in their fireplace.

Laura's father was sentenced to the state's maximum term of sixteen years in prison and will be registered as a sex offender indefinitely. Their lawyers are attempting to tack on a civil suit against him due to the mental anguish he caused his wife and daughters. They are pleased that it is mandatory for him, as a sex offender, to participate in psychological therapy sessions due to his sexual misconduct with an underage family member.

Elise, Janine, and Cassie were all desperate for a *human* friend and formed a close relationship with each other shortly after their own stories were revealed. Elise and Cassie have also befriended Janine's dog, Blue, and the four of them get together nearly every day. At the assembly, the three of them met numerous other students who had either fallen prey to cyber relationships or also felt intimidated due to their own lack of self-esteem. Janine, Elise, and Cassie will never feel alone and unwanted again, and neither will their newfound mix of friends they eagerly hang around with.

Cassie was even contacted by a cute boy her age who lives two towns over. He had seen the presentation she made at the assembly and claims he is just as tall and as socially inept as she is. They plan on meeting each other before they attend his high school holiday dance together but are satisfied doing FaceTime calls with each other every day for the time being. Neither one can recall a time when they felt so happy and so *normal*.

Barry sent Carrie's parents a copy of his assembly video with another apology. They haven't completely forgiven him for introducing drugs to their daughter, but after seeing his story detailing how one mistake can ruin everything, they are both working on repairing their once-close relationship with him and his family. All of them have even begun planning a visit to Carrie together in the near future. Barry was relieved to hear the police have arrested his brother's ex-friend for resisting arrest, dealing mass quantities of drugs, knowingly distributing tainted drugs, distributing to minors, and possession of drugs on school property with the intent to distribute. Barry hopes to testify on behalf of himself and Carrie before the judge passes down his sentence.

All of Claire's remaining fifteen students felt so proud and justified after putting on their assembly. Any lingering doubts they may have had prior are completely forgotten. The positive results the fifteen classmates experienced from that day forward has been more rewarding than they ever dreamed possible. Each one of them was approached by other students after the assembly to voice a similar story creating a shared bond between them forever. Not only did they help countless others, but also their own self-worth skyrocketed, and so did their grades and overall happiness.

One of the greatest successes achieved, however, was the profound effect their assembly had on a group of students who were notorious for being the biggest bullies in school. After speaking with Claire and some of her students after the assembly, these tormentors started telling their own traumatic stories about parental, relative, and sibling abuse they have had to endure for years and were unfortunately taking out their pain and frustration on other students—until now. Since the bullying has all but stopped, the entire school seems to have a renewed sense of pride and respect for others as never seen before. Cory and Dave no longer need to look over their shoulder or worry about their locker doors slamming shut. Both teens are still dealing with depression but are learning to deal with their issues one step at a time.

A positive effect has also taken place on all of the parents who attended the assembly. They are learning to be more accepting and cognizant of their teenager's feelings as well as their own parenting faults.

Several clips from their school assembly went viral, and school districts and libraries across the country have ordered a copy of their entire presentation. All the proceeds they earn from their orders go directly into the Toni Marchand Memorial Foundation helping crisis centers for teenagers across the country. Emily's rapist's father was the first to donate to the memorial foundation. He contributed fifty thousand dollars to aid teen rape victims but also toward treatments for teens with compulsive sexual behavior and sex addictions like his son.

Claire's remaining fifteen students no longer have trouble fitting in at school. They have each taken Toni's words to heart and are truly grateful for their special gift of life and are trying to live each day without wasting another minute.

Their scars will always be there, but their wounds have finally healed.

The End

About the Author

Patti Olson grew up in Batavia, Illinois, a western suburb of Chicago. After attending Augustana College in Rock Island and Moser School in Chicago, she married Bart Neri from Geneva, Illinois, in 1975.

Family meant everything, and continuing their ancestors' traditions was a privilege for both Bart and Patti to uphold. Now their children, Mike and his partner, Janet; Joe and his wife, Beth; and grandchildren, Juliann and Tommy, have carried on those family traditions.

Throughout her married life, Patti worked as an executive secretary, a salesclerk, a Realtor, a caregiver, and a golf starter, to name a few. She was always volunteering for their church, sons' schools, and Cub Scouts.

After retirement, Patti and Bart moved to Florida and enjoyed a leisurely life of golf carts and nonstop entertainment in The Villages until Bart's passing in 2019. Patti missed living in the Midwest and moved to Oxford, Ohio, in 2023. She loves the quaintness of a small college town with all the cultural offerings and diversity of a big city.

Patti's talents evolved throughout the years, from designing an enticing silent auction gift basket or writing a new skit for a Scout troop to her revered edible creations and memorable holiday parties. But once she began using her creativity for writing short stories, novels, and animated screenplays, Patti found her true passion.

Within each of the author's works, at least one truth about Patti has been included on its pages. The story may be based on a past personal experience or center on one of her most cherished family keepsakes or something as trivial as a single charm on her favorite necklace. Including a piece of herself within her works has become her own personal trademark.

Printed in the USA
CPSIA information can be obtained
at www.ICGtesting.com
CBHW031359061224
18487CB00045B/542